THE COMPLETE DIABETES DIET COOKBOOK

Over 100 Nutrient-Packed Recipes for Managing Diabetes, Promoting Wellness, and Boosting Energy while Managing Blood Sugar and Weight.

FRANCIS E. SAGER

Copyright © 2024 Francis E. Sager

Protected under copyright law. No component of this publication might be reproduced, put away in a recovery framework, or Communicated in any Structure or utilizing any And all methods, Electronic, mechanical, copying, recording, etc. Without the earlier composed Consent of the copyright owners, With the exception of short Citations Utilized in basic surveys or publications.

TABLE OF CONTENTS

- INTRODUCTION 7
- UNDERSTANDING DIABETES 8
- KEY CONCEPTS IN DIABETES: 9
- MANAGEMENT OF DIABETES: 9
- BASICS OF DIABETIC NUTRITION 10
- BUILDING A BALANCED PLATE 12
- GLYCEMIC INDEX AND GLYCEMIC LOAD 13
- UNDERSTANDING THE IMPACT ON BLOOD SUGAR 15
- ESSENTIAL NUTRIENTS FOR DIABETICS 16
- KITCHEN ESSENTIALS FOR DIABETIC COOKING 18
- ESSENTIAL INGREDIENTS 20
- SHOPPING TIPS FOR DIABETIC-FRIENDLY FOODS 22
- DELICIOUS BREAKFAST 25
- Greek Yogurt Parfait 25
- Oatmeal with Fresh Fruit 26
- Vegetable Omelette 27
- Whole Grain Toast with Avocado 28
- Cottage Cheese and Pineapple Bowl 29
- Chia Seed Pudding 30
- Quinoa Breakfast Bowl 31
- Smoothie Bowl 32
- Egg and Vegetable Wrap 33
- Sweet Potato Hash 34
- Whole Wheat Pancakes with Berries 35
- Salmon and Cream Cheese Bagel 36
- Almond Flour Waffles 37
- Veggie Breakfast Burrito 38
- Muesli with Yogurt 39
- Egg Muffins 40
- Peanut Butter and Banana Sandwich 41
- Coconut Flour Porridge 42
- Avocado and Tomato Toast 43
- Berry and Spinach Smoothie 44
- WHOLESOME LUNCH 45
- Grilled Chicken Salad 45
- Quinoa and Black Bean Bowl 46
- Salmon and Vegetable Stir-Fry 47
- Turkey and Hummus Wrap 48
- Mediterranean Chickpea Salad 49
- Vegetable and Tofu Stir-Fry 50
- Caprese Chicken Salad 51
- Whole Wheat Pasta with Pesto and Vegetables 52
- Shrimp and Avocado Lettuce Wraps 53
- Stuffed Bell Peppers 54
- DINNER IDEAS 55
- Grilled Chicken Breast with Roasted Vegetables 55
- Salmon and Asparagus Foil Packets 56
- Vegetarian Quinoa Stir-Fry 57
- Turkey and Vegetable Skewers 58
- Cauliflower Fried Rice with Shrimp 59
- Lemon Herb Baked Cod with Sweet Potato Mash 60
- Chickpea and Spinach Curry 61
- Stuffed Bell Peppers with Ground Turkey . 62
- Eggplant and Zucchini Lasagna 63
- Beef and Vegetable Stir-Fry with Brown Rice 64
- QUICK AND EASY SNACKS 65
- Greek Yogurt with Berries 65

Vegetable Sticks with Hummus 66
Hard-Boiled Eggs 67
Nuts and Seeds Mix 68
Cheese and Whole Grain Crackers 69
Apple Slices with Peanut Butter 70
Cottage Cheese with Pineapple 71
Yogurt Parfait 72
Cherry Tomatoes with Mozzarella 73
Avocado and Whole Grain Toast 74

BEVERAGES 75
Cinnamon Tea 75
Hibiscus Tea 75
Green Tea 76
Green Power Juice 76
Berry Protein Smoothie with Unsweetened Soy Milk 77
Turmeric Ginger Latte with Unsweetened Coconut Milk 77
Simple Coconut Water 78
Spiced Coconut Water 78
Coconut Water Smoothie 79
Sparkling Coconut Water 79

DESERT 80
Fruit Salad with Mint 80
Baked Pears with Cinnamon and Walnuts 81
Dark Chocolate-Dipped Banana Slices 82
Chia Seed Pudding Parfait 83
Frozen Yogurt Bark 84
Coconut and Almond Energy Bites 85
Baked Cinnamon Apple Slices 86
Homemade Berry Sorbet 87
Avocado Chocolate Mousse 88
Yogurt Parfait with Granola 89

SALAD 90
Classic Greek Salad 90
Quinoa and Vegetable Salad 91
Chicken Caesar Salad 92
Mango Avocado Salad 93
Caprese Salad 94
Asian Sesame Chicken Salad 95
Spinach and Strawberry Salad 96
Cobb Salad 97
Mediterranean Chickpea Salad 98
Taco Salad 99

FISH AND SEAFOOD 100
Grilled Salmon with Lemon and Dill 100
Shrimp Scampi 101
Baked Cod with Herbs 102
Cajun Spiced Tilapia 103
Lemon Garlic Butter Shrimp 104
Tuna Steak Salad 105
Garlic Herb Grilled Swordfish 106
Coconut Curry Shrimp 107
Baked Lemon Garlic Butter Scallops 108
Miso Glazed Grilled Sea Bass 109

POULTRY 110
Grilled Lemon Herb Chicken 110
Baked Garlic Parmesan Turkey Meatballs 111
Rosemary Roasted Chicken Thighs 112
Lemon Garlic Herb Turkey Breast 113
Cilantro Lime Grilled Chicken 114
Pesto Baked Chicken 115
Sesame Ginger Chicken Stir-Fry 116
Honey Mustard Glazed Chicken 117
Herb-Roasted Quail 118
Greek Yogurt Marinated Chicken Skewers 119

- BEEF AND PORK 120
- Grilled Sirloin Steak with Herb Marinade 120
- Beef and Vegetable Stir-Fry 121
- Zucchini Noodles with Beef Bolognese .. 122
- Mexican Beef Lettuce Wraps 123
- Grilled Pork Tenderloin with Mustard Glaze 124
- Baked Pork Chops with Apple Chutney.. 125
- Pork and Vegetable Stir-Fry 126
- Pork and Spinach Stuffed Mushrooms ... 127
- Beef and Broccoli Stir-Fry 128
- MEAL PLAN 129
- DINING OUT 130
- SOCIAL GATHERINGS 131
- THANKSGIVING DINNER MENU 132
- Roasted Vegetable Platter with Yogurt Dip 132
- Herb-Roasted Turkey Breast 133
- Quinoa and Cranberry Stuffed Acorn Squash 134
- Mashed Cauliflower 136
- Pumpkin Chia Pudding Parfait 137
- CHRISTMAS DINNER MENU 138
- Smoked Salmon Cucumber Bites 138
- Balsamic Glazed Roast Beef 139
- Herb-Roasted Brussels sprouts 140
- Cauliflower and Broccoli Gratin 141
- Spinach and Pomegranate Salad 142
- Sugar-Free Berry Trifle 143
- BIRTHDAY CELEBRATION MENU 144
- Caprese Skewers 144
- Grilled Chicken with Lemon-Herb Marinade 145
- Cauliflower Rice Pilaf 146
- Roasted Asparagus with Parmesan 147
- Quinoa Salad with Feta and Cherry Tomatoes 148
- Sugar-Free Cheesecake with Berry Compote 149
- NEW YEAR'S EVE CELEBRATION 150
- Spicy Shrimp Ceviche with Citrus and Herbs 150
- Herb-Crusted Salmon Fillets 151
- Zucchini Noodles with Pesto 152
- Roasted Balsamic Brussels sprouts 153
- Quinoa and Kale Stuffed Bell Peppers ... 154
- Dark Chocolate-Dipped Strawberries 155
- LIFESTYLE AND EXERCISE 156
- LIFESTYLE TIPS 156
- INCORPORATING PHYSICAL ACTIVITY INTO DAILY LIFE 158
- CONCLUSION 160
- FREQUENTLY ASKED QUESTIONS 161
- GLOSSARY 164

INTRODUCTION

In the complex fabric of our lives, one thread stands out clearly - our health. The decisions we make regarding our food play a key role in determining the course of our well-being, and for those controlling diabetes, this becomes an even more critical part of daily life. "The Complete Diabetes Diet Cookbook," is a complete guide meant to encourage people with diabetes to not only control their condition but to accept a lifestyle rich in delicious, healthy, and balanced meals.

The frequency of diabetes has hit staggering levels worldwide, making it one of the most important health issues of our time. However, managing diabetes doesn't mean losing the joy of eating or settling on taste. This guide is more than a mere collection of recipes; it is a cooking trip designed to meet the unique dietary needs of people living with diabetes, providing them with the tools and information to make informed decisions about their nutrition.

Within these pages, you will find a treasure trove of recipes carefully created to cater to different food choices, including vegetarian, vegan, and gluten-free options. The focus is not just on the limit but on accepting a varied and colorful array of foods that not only balance blood sugar levels but also delight the taste buds.

"The Complete Diabetes Diet Cookbook" is not just about what to eat; it's a guide that goes into the 'how' and 'why' behind every dish. It demystifies the complex world of nutrition, breaking down the science behind the ingredients to help readers understand how certain foods can impact their blood sugar levels. By providing people with information, this recipe aims to create a sense of liberty and confidence in making food choices that match with their health goals.

Beyond the meals, this guide serves as a partner on the path to overall well-being. It addresses the intersection of thoughtful eating, exercise, and stress management, understanding that controlling diabetes is not a one-size-fits-all method. By adding a complete viewpoint, it supports a lifestyle that goes beyond the plate, supporting general health and energy.

The culinary scene presented within these pages is a celebration of the variety of tastes and foods from around the world. From hearty breakfasts to filling lunches, sumptuous dinners, and tempting desserts, every recipe is a testament to the notion that controlling diabetes can be a culinary adventure rather than a limit.

As you start on this cooking adventure with "The Complete Diabetes Diet Cookbook," let it be a lesson that delicious, healthy meals are not just a necessity but a happy part of a lively and fulfilling life. Here's to enjoying every bite, feeding the body, and thriving on the road towards a better, happy you.

UNDERSTANDING DIABETES

Diabetes mellitus, generally referred to as diabetes, is a chronic metabolic illness characterized by increased amounts of glucose (sugar) in the blood. This disorder comes from the body's failure to generate enough insulin, a hormone that plays a critical role in controlling blood sugar, or the inability of the body's cells to react adequately to insulin.

There are various forms of diabetes, with the two major groups being Type 1 and Type 2 diabetes:

TYPE 1 DIABETES:

Cause: Type 1 diabetes is an autoimmune disorder where the immune system erroneously assaults and kills insulin-producing cells in the pancreas. The specific etiology of this immunological response is not entirely known, however, it is considered to include a mix of hereditary and environmental variables.

Onset: It commonly develops early in life, often during infancy or adolescence.
Treatment: Individuals with Type 1 diabetes must take insulin via injections or an insulin pump to maintain their blood sugar levels.

TYPE 2 DIABETES:

Cause: Type 2 diabetes is characterized by insulin resistance, where the body's cells may not react effectively to insulin, and the pancreas may not generate enough insulin to satisfy the increasing demand. Lifestyle factors, genetics, and obesity are key contributors to the development of Type 2 diabetes.

Onset: It normally develops in maturity, although an increasing number of instances are also being detected in younger persons.
Treatment: Lifestyle adjustments, including dietary changes, frequent physical exercise, and medication (oral or injectable), are typically advised to control Type 2 diabetes.

GESTATIONAL DIABETES:

Cause: This kind of diabetes happens during pregnancy when the body cannot manufacture enough insulin to satisfy the increasing needs. It may raise the chance of difficulties for both the mother and the baby.

Onset: Typically diagnosed during the second or third trimester of pregnancy.
Treatment: Monitoring blood sugar levels, dietary modifications, and, in certain situations, insulin treatment may be necessary.

KEY CONCEPTS IN DIABETES:

Insulin: Produced by the pancreas, insulin is a hormone responsible for controlling blood sugar levels. It helps cells to absorb glucose for energy.

Glucose: This is the major source of energy for the body. It originates from the food we consume, mainly carbs.

Hyperglycemia: Elevated blood sugar levels. This illness, if left mismanaged, may develop into different issues affecting the heart, kidneys, eyes, and nerves.

Hypoglycemia: Abnormally low blood sugar levels, generally a consequence of too much insulin or certain drugs.

Complications: Prolonged untreated diabetes may lead to major health complications such as cardiovascular illnesses, renal difficulties, nerve damage, and eye impairment.

MANAGEMENT OF DIABETES:

Lifestyle Modifications: Adopting a nutritious diet, participating in regular physical exercise, keeping a healthy weight, and avoiding tobacco use are key components of diabetes treatment.

Medication: Depending on the type of diabetes, medication may be provided to regulate blood sugar levels. This may include oral medicines, injectable insulin, or other injectable treatments that assist manage glucose.

Monitoring: Regular monitoring of blood sugar levels is crucial for those with diabetes. This may be done using blood glucose meters, continuous glucose monitors (CGMs), or other monitoring equipment.

Education and Support: Understanding diabetes and learning how to manage it is a constant journey. Diabetes education programs and support groups serve a critical role in encouraging patients to take control of their health.

A proactive and comprehensive approach to controlling diabetes comprises a mix of medical treatment, lifestyle modifications, and continual education. With careful treatment, persons with diabetes may enjoy full and active lives while limiting the risk of complications associated with the illness.

BASICS OF DIABETIC NUTRITION

Carbohydrate Management:

- Carbohydrates have the greatest direct influence on blood sugar levels. It's crucial to monitor and regulate carbohydrate consumption.
- Choose complex carbs with a low glycemic index (GI) since they induce a slower increase in blood sugar. Examples include whole grains, legumes, and non-starchy veggies.
- Portion control is key. Balancing carbohydrate consumption with protein and healthy fats may help minimize rises in blood sugar.

Fiber-Rich Foods:

- Foods rich in fiber, such as whole grains, fruits, vegetables, and legumes, are excellent for persons with diabetes.
- Fiber helps manage blood sugar levels, promotes fullness, and supports digestive health.

Protein Sources:

- Include lean protein sources in your diet, such as chicken, fish, tofu, lentils, and low-fat dairy products.
- Protein helps balance blood sugar levels and provides a sensation of fullness.

Healthy Fats:

- Choose sources of healthful fats, like avocados, nuts, seeds, and olive oil.
- Limit saturated and Tran's fats found in fried meals, processed snacks, and fatty cuts of meat.

Meal Timing and Regularity:

- Establish a regular food pattern with properly spaced meals and snacks.
- Avoid missing meals, since this might contribute to swings in blood sugar levels.

Portion Control:

- Be cautious of portion sizes to prevent overeating, which may alter blood sugar levels and lead to weight gain.
- Use smaller plates and utensils to help regulate servings.

Limit Added Sugars:

- Minimize the consumption of foods and beverages rich in added sugars, such as sugary drinks, sweets, and desserts.
- Read product labels to detect hidden sources of sugar in processed meals.

Hydration:

- Stay well-hydrated with water or other low-calorie drinks.
- Limit the intake of sugary beverages, since they may quickly elevate blood sugar levels.

Regular Monitoring:

- Monitor blood sugar levels periodically to learn how various foods and meals affect your body.
- Work with healthcare specialists to develop individualized blood sugar objectives.

Individualized Approach:

- Diabetic nutrition is not one-size-fits-all. Individualize your nutrition depending on personal tastes, cultural factors, and lifestyle.
- Consult with a qualified dietician or healthcare practitioner to build a tailored dietary plan.

Balanced and Varied Diet:

- Aim for a balanced and diverse diet that includes a broad variety of nutrient-dense foods.
- Include a variety of colored fruits and vegetables to guarantee a wide spectrum of nutrients.

Physical Activity:

- Regular physical exercise is a vital aspect of diabetes care. It helps enhance insulin sensitivity and improves general health.

- Engage in things you love, and strive for a mix of aerobic activity and strength training.

BUILDING A BALANCED PLATE

Building a balanced plate is a vital facet of maintaining overall health and well-being, especially for persons managing diabetes. A well-constructed plate helps maintain blood sugar levels, supplies important nutrients, and promotes energy balance. Here's guidance on making a balanced meal, customized to the special requirements of persons with diabetes:

1. Fill Half Your Plate with Non-Starchy Vegetables: Examples: Broccoli, spinach, kale, bell peppers, cauliflower, and zucchini.
Why: Non-starchy veggies are rich in fiber, vitamins, and minerals. They have a modest influence on blood sugar levels and provide heft to your meals, increasing fullness.

2. Quarter of Your Plate with Lean Proteins: Examples: Chicken, turkey, fish, tofu, lentils, eggs.
Why: Protein helps balance blood sugar levels, maintains muscular function, and delivers a sensation of fullness. Choose lean protein sources to decrease saturated fats.

3. Quarter of Your Plate with Whole Grains or Starchy Vegetables: Examples: Quinoa, brown rice, sweet potatoes, whole-grain pasta, lentils.
Why: Whole grains and starchy vegetables give a constant flow of energy, and their fiber content assists with blood sugar regulation. Opt for whole, less processed products.

4. Incorporate Healthy Fats: Examples: Avocado, almonds, seeds, olive oil.
Why: Healthy fats are crucial for heart health and may help regulate appetite. Be aware of portion proportions, since fats are calorie-dense.

5. Include Dairy or Dairy substitutes: Examples: Low-fat or fat-free yogurt, milk, or fortified plant-based substitutes.
Why: Dairy products supply calcium and vitamin D for bone health. Choose low-fat choices to manage saturated fat consumption.

6. Mindful Carbohydrate Choices: Examples: Choose healthy grains, legumes, and modest servings of fruits.
Why: Carbohydrates alter blood sugar levels, therefore it's crucial to pick complex, high-fiber choices. Portion control is crucial.

7. Watch Portions:
Why: Controlling portion sizes helps regulate calorie intake, reducing overconsumption. Use smaller dishes and bowls to promote proper servings.

8. Stay Hydrated: Drink water throughout the day.
Why: Staying hydrated is vital for overall wellness. Water does not affect blood sugar levels and helps with digestion.

9. Limit Added Sugars: Read food labels and be careful of added sugars in processed foods.
Why: Excessive sugar consumption might lead to blood sugar increases. Choose complete, naturally sweet meals over sugary snacks and drinks.

10. Consider the Glycemic Index:
Be careful of the glycemic index (GI) of foods.
Why: The GI evaluates how rapidly a meal boosts blood sugar levels. Choosing low-GI meals may help regulate blood sugar.

11. Regular Physical Activity: Incorporate regular exercise into your regimen.
Why: Physical exercise increases insulin sensitivity, helps control weight, and promotes general health.

12. Consult with Healthcare Professionals: Work with a licensed dietician or healthcare practitioner.
Why: They can give individualized advice based on your unique health requirements and nutritional choices.

GLYCEMIC INDEX AND GLYCEMIC LOAD

The Glycemic Index (GI) and Glycemic Load (GL) are methods used to quantify the influence of carbohydrate-containing diets on blood sugar levels. These principles are especially essential for those managing diabetes since they aid in making educated decisions regarding the kinds and quantities of carbs eaten.

GLYCEMIC INDEX (GI):

1. Definition:

The Glycemic Index (GI) is a numerical scale that assesses carbohydrate-containing meals based on how rapidly they elevate blood sugar levels.

2. Scale:

The scale normally spans from 0 to 100.
Foods having a high GI (70 or higher) induce a quick surge in blood sugar.
Foods with a medium GI (56-69) result in a modest rise in blood sugar.
Low-GI meals (55 or below) have a slower, more progressive influence on blood sugar.

3. Determining Factors:

The kind of carbohydrate and its structure determine the GI.
Simple carbs, such as those found in sweet meals, tend to have a higher GI.
Complex carbs, including those in whole grains and legumes, often have a lower GI.

4. Examples:

High-GI Foods: White bread, sugary cereals, baked potatoes.
Medium-GI Foods: Brown rice, oatmeal, whole wheat bread.
Low-GI Foods: Quinoa, lentils, most non-starchy veggies.

5. Usefulness:

The GI is a valuable tool for analyzing individual foods but may not account for the effect of mixed meals or portion sizes.

GLYCEMIC LOAD (GL):

1. Definition:

Glycemic Load (GL) is a metric that combines the quality and amount of carbs in a given portion of food, offering a more realistic picture of its influence on blood sugar.

2. Calculation:

GL is computed by multiplying the GI of a meal by the number of accessible carbs in a serving and dividing the result by 100.
Formula: $GL = (GI \times Carbohydrate\, content\, in\, grams) / 100$

3. Scale:

Low GL (10 or below): Low influence on blood sugar.
Moderate GL (11-19): Moderate effect.
High GL (20 or above): High influence on blood sugar.

4. Usefulness:

GL takes into consideration both the quality and amount of carbs, offering a more realistic way to assess the influence of a given diet on blood sugar levels.

5. Examples:

Watermelon has a high GI but a low GL per serving since it contains comparatively little carbs.
A big serving of French fries may have a high GL owing to both its high GI and the hefty carbohydrate content.

UNDERSTANDING THE IMPACT ON BLOOD SUGAR

The impact of food on blood sugar levels is a critical consideration for individuals, especially those managing diabetes. Both the Glycemic Index (GI) and Glycemic Load (GL) play a crucial role in predicting how different foods affect blood sugar. Here's an overview of how these factors influence blood sugar levels:

GLYCEMIC INDEX (GI):

High GI Foods:

- **Impact**: Foods with a high GI cause a rapid spike in blood sugar levels.
- **Examples**: White bread, sugary cereals, and baked potatoes.
- **Considerations**: High-GI foods are quickly digested and absorbed, leading to a swift increase in blood glucose.

Medium GI Foods:

- **Impact**: Foods with a medium GI result in a moderate increase in blood sugar.
- **Examples**: Brown rice, oatmeal, and whole wheat bread.
- **Considerations**: These foods have a slower impact on blood sugar compared to high-GI foods.

Low GI Foods:

- **Impact**: Foods with a low GI have a slower, more gradual effect on blood sugar levels.
- **Examples**: Quinoa, lentils, and most non-starchy vegetables.
- **Considerations**: Low-GI foods are digested and absorbed slowly, leading to a slower rise in blood glucose.

GLYCEMIC LOAD (GL):

Low GL Foods:

- **Impact**: Low-GL foods have a minimal impact on blood sugar levels.
- **Examples**: Most non-starchy vegetables, certain fruits in moderation.
- **Considerations**: Even foods with a high GI can have a low GL if the portion size is small.

Moderate GL Foods:

- **Impact**: Moderate-GL foods have a moderate effect on blood sugar levels.
- **Examples**: Whole grains, legumes, and some fruits.
- **Considerations**: Balancing higher-GI foods with fiber and nutrients can moderate their impact on blood glucose.

High GL Foods:

- **Impact**: High-GL foods can cause a significant increase in blood sugar levels.
- **Examples**: Processed foods, sugary snacks, and large portions of high-GI foods.
- **Considerations**: Monitoring portion sizes and combining them with other nutrients can help mitigate the impact on blood glucose.

ESSENTIAL NUTRIENTS FOR DIABETICS

Individuals with diabetes need to pay special attention to their food intake to maintain blood sugar levels and promote overall health. Here are key nutrients that play a critical part in the well-being of persons with diabetes:

1. **Fiber**: Role: Fiber assists in blood sugar regulation by delaying the digestion and absorption of carbs.
Sources: Whole grains, fruits, vegetables, legumes, nuts, and seeds.

2. **Protein**: Role: Protein helps maintain muscular mass, maintains satiety, and has a low influence on blood sugar levels.

Sources: Lean meats, poultry, fish, tofu, legumes, dairy products, and plant-based protein sources.

3. **Healthy Fats**: Role: Healthy fats help to heart health and give prolonged energy.
Sources: Avocado, nuts, seeds, olive oil, fatty seafood (like salmon and mackerel).
4. **Omega-3 Fatty Acids**: Role: Omega-3s have anti-inflammatory characteristics and may help lower the risk of cardiovascular problems linked with diabetes.
Sources: Fatty fish, chia seeds, flaxseeds, walnuts.

5. **Vitamins and Minerals**:

Vitamin D: Supports bone health and may have a function in insulin sensitivity.
Sources: Sunlight, fatty fish, enriched dairy products.

Magnesium: Important for glucose metabolism.
Sources: Nuts, seeds, leafy green veggies, whole grains.

Vitamin B12: Essential for nerve health.
Sources: Animal products (meat, dairy), fortified plant-based substitutes.

6. **Chromium**: Role: Chromium improves the effect of insulin.
Sources: Whole grains, broccoli, almonds, and some meats.

7. **Antioxidants**: Role: Protect cells from oxidative stress, which is exacerbated in diabetes.
Sources: Berries, dark chocolate, almonds, leafy green veggies.

8. **Calcium**: Role: Important for bone health and neurological function.
Sources: Dairy products, fortified plant-based milk, leafy green vegetables.

9. **Potassium**: Role: Helps control blood pressure.
Sources: Bananas, oranges, tomatoes, potatoes, leafy green veggies.

10. **Water**: Role: Adequate hydration is vital for general health and may help regulate blood sugar levels.
Sources: Water, herbal teas, and other low-calorie liquids.

11. **Carbs with Low Glycemic Index**: Role: Choosing carbs with a low glycemic index may help regulate blood sugar levels.
Sources: Whole grains, legumes, non-starchy veggies.

12. **Probiotics**: Role: Supports gut health, which may impact metabolic health.
Sources: Yogurt, kefir, sauerkraut, kimchi.

13. **Coenzyme Q10 (CoQ10)**: Role: Antioxidant that may offer advantages for cardiovascular health.
Sources: Fish, meat, nuts, and certain oils.

14. **Folate (Vitamin B9)**: Role: Supports cell division and may lessen the incidence of cardiovascular problems.
Sources: Leafy green vegetables, beans, fortified cereals.

15. **Cinnamon**: Role: Some research shows that cinnamon may have insulin-sensitizing characteristics.
Sources: Sprinkle on meals or include in recipes.

KITCHEN ESSENTIALS FOR DIABETIC COOKING

Creating a diabetes-friendly kitchen entails having the necessary equipment, products, and a well-organized area to encourage healthy cooking and eating habits. Here are some kitchen requirements for diabetic cooking:

1. **Measuring Tools**: Measuring Cups and Spoons: Accurate portion management is vital for maintaining blood sugar levels.

2. **Food Scale**: Digital Scale: Helps measure items correctly, particularly for portion management and carbohydrate counting.

3. **Cutting Tools**: Chef's Knife and Cutting Board: Essential for slicing vegetables, fruits, and other materials.
Vegetable Peeler: Useful for peeling fruits and vegetables.

4. **Cooking Appliances**: High-excellent Cookware: Non-stick pans, stainless steel pots, and excellent baking sheets for healthy cooking.
Slow Cooker or Instant Pot: Convenient for producing healthful, slow-cooked meals.

5. **Blender or Food Processor**: Blender: Ideal for creating smoothies, soups, and sauces with entire fruits and vegetables.
Food Processor: Useful for chopping, slicing, and prepping different items.

6. **Non-Starchy veggies**: Variety of Fresh and Frozen Vegetables: Stock up on non-starchy veggies including broccoli, spinach, peppers, and cauliflower.

7. **Whole Grains and Legumes**: Quinoa, Brown Rice, Lentils, and Whole-Grain Pasta: Rich in fiber and complex carbs.

8. **Lean Proteins**: Skinless Poultry, Fish, Tofu, and Legumes: Excellent sources of lean protein with low influence on blood sugar.

9. **Healthy Fats**: Olive Oil, Avocado, Nuts, and Seeds: Incorporate them into meals and salads for healthy fats.

10. **Low-Sodium Broths and Stocks**: Vegetable and Chicken Broths: Useful for preparing tasty and low-calorie soups.

11. **Herbs and Spices**: Variety of Herbs and Spices: Enhance taste without adding salt or sugar.

12. **Low-salt Sauces and Condiments**: Low-sodium soy Sauce, Mustard, and Vinegar: Flavorful alternatives with lower salt content.

13. **Sugar Alternatives**: Stevia, Monk Fruit, or Erythritol: Non-nutritive sweeteners for people who wish to reduce additional sugars.

14. **Whole Fruit**: Fresh and Frozen Fruits: Choose whole fruits with lower glycemic index values.

15. **Dairy or Dairy Alternatives**: Low-fat or Fat-Free Yogurt and Milk: Good sources of calcium and protein.

16. **Nut Butter**: Natural Peanut Butter or Almond Butter: A good source of protein and lipids.

17. **High-Fiber Cereals and Oats**: Whole Grain Cereals and Rolled Oats: High-fiber alternatives for a healthful breakfast.

18. **Nutritional Labels**: Reading Glasses: If required, read nutritional labels and ingredient lists efficiently.

19. **Storage Containers**: Containers for Meal Prep: Make it simple to store and portion food for the week.

20. **Water Filtration System**: Water Pitcher or Filtration System: Encourages hydration without extra sweets.

21. **Blood Glucose Monitor**: Blood Glucose Monitor and Strips: Essential for frequent monitoring and keeping awareness of blood sugar levels.

22. **Notebook or Meal Planner**: Notebook or Meal Planner: Keep track of meals, snacks, and blood sugar levels.

23. **Emergency Snacks**: Healthy Snacks: Keep nuts, seeds, or whole-grain crackers on hand for emergency snacks.

24. **Supportive Cookbooks**: Diabetes-Friendly Cookbooks: Explore recipes intended for persons managing diabetes.

25. **Comfortable Shoes or Anti-weariness Mats**: Comfortable Footwear or Anti-Fatigue Mats: For people who spend lengthy times in the kitchen, boosting comfort and minimizing weariness.

ESSENTIAL INGREDIENTS

The main components for diabetic-friendly cooking should be concentrated nutrient-dense foods that promote general health and assist control of blood sugar levels. Below is a summary of the necessary ingredients:

1. **Whole Grains**: Rich in fiber and complex carbs, whole wheat pasta, quinoa, barley, and brown rice provide you with long-lasting energy.

2. **Lean Proteins**: Turkey, Fish, Tofu, Skinless Chicken, and Legumes: Excellent protein sources that have little effect on blood sugar levels.

3. **Non-Starchy Vegetables**: Low in carbs and high in fiber, vitamins, and minerals including broccoli, spinach, kale, bell peppers, and cauliflower.

4. **Good Fats**: Nuts, seeds, avocado, olive oil: These foods provide necessary fatty acids and aid in fullness.

5. **Low-Fat Dairy or Dairy Alternatives**: Almond milk, Greek yogurt, and skim milk are healthy options that are low in fat and high in protein and calcium.

6. **Fresh and Frozen Fruits**: Berries, Apples, and Citrus Fruits: Select fruits with modest quantities and lower glycemic index values.

7. **Whole Eggs**: An adaptable source of protein that can be cooked in a variety of ways.

8. **Legumes**: Black beans, chickpeas, and lentils are high in protein and fiber and hence great options for regulating blood sugar.

9. **Herbs and Spices**: Add flavor without adding sugar or salt using cinnamon, turmeric, basil, and rosemary.

10. **Whole Nuts and Seeds**: Chia Seeds, Flaxseeds, Walnuts, and Almonds: These foods include fiber, vital nutrients, and healthy fats.

11. **High-Fiber Cereals and Oats**: For a wholesome breakfast, choose high-fiber alternatives like Bran Cereals and Steel-Cut Oats.

12. **Vegetable and Chicken Broths**: Useful for making tasty, low-calorie soups; low-sodium broths and stocks.

13. **Low-Sodium Sauces & Condiments**: savory selections with a lower sodium concentration include low-sodium soy sauce, mustard, and vinegar.

14. Use whole grain flour, such as almond and whole wheat flour, in baking to boost the fiber content.

15. **Sugar Substitutes**: Erythritol, Monk Fruit, and Stevia: Non-nutritive sweeteners for those who want to reduce their intake of added sugar.

16. **Onions and Garlic**: Onions, Garlic, Shallots: Add flavor without adding extra sugar, salt, or calories.

17. **Low-Fat Cheese**: Cottage cheese, Feta, and part-skim mozzarella are all excellent sources of protein and calcium with less fat.

18. **Whole Wheat or Whole Grain Tortillas or Wraps**: Use as a healthier substitute for regular tortillas or wraps in sandwiches.

19. **Vinegar**: Apple cider and balsamic Vinegar: Give food some tang without adding any more sweetness.

20. **Dark chocolate (moderate consumption)**: Dark chocolate (70% cocoa or more) is a delicacy that, when ingested in moderation, may have health advantages.

21. **Whole Grain Mustard**: A tasty condiment with a little texture added.

22. **Flavored Extracts**: Add flavor to food without adding extra calories using vanilla, almond, or lemon extract.

23. **Unsweetened Applesauce**: This natural sweetener may be used in place of fats in baking.

24. **Low-Fat Salad Dressings**: Olive oil vinaigrettes: Use sparingly for marinades and salads.
25. **Products Made From Tomatoes**: Tomato paste and canned tomatoes are adaptable components for stews, soups, and sauces.

SHOPPING TIPS FOR DIABETIC-FRIENDLY FOODS

Shopping for diabetic-friendly foods entails making careful decisions to promote blood sugar management and general health. Here are some shopping tips to help you make educated judgments when traversing the grocery store:

1. **Plan Before You Go**:
   - Create a Shopping List: Plan your meals and snacks for the week, then build a shopping list based on your planned dishes.

   - Stick to the List: Avoid impulsive purchases by adhering to your pre-planned list.

2. **Shop the Perimeter**:
   - Fresh Produce Section: Load up on fresh fruits and veggies, since they are full of fiber, vitamins, and minerals.
   - Lean Proteins: Visit the meat or seafood counter for lean protein sources such as chicken, fish, and tofu.
   - Dairy or Dairy Alternatives: Choose low-fat or fat-free alternatives from the dairy area.

3. **Read Food Labels**:
   - Check Nutritional Information: Pay attention to total carbs, fiber, and added sugars on food labels.
   - Serving Sizes: Be cautious of serving sizes to appropriately determine the influence on blood sugar levels.

4. **Choose Whole Grains**:
   - Opt for Whole Grains: Choose whole grains like brown rice, quinoa, and whole wheat pasta over processed grains.
   - Check Labels for Fiber Content: Higher fiber content is useful for blood sugar regulation.

5. **Prioritize Lean Proteins**:
   - Select Lean Cuts: Choose lean cuts of meat and poultry to limit saturated fat consumption.

- Include Plant-Based Proteins: Incorporate tofu, lentils, and plant-based protein sources for diversity.

6. **Include Healthy Fats**:
   - Select Healthy Cooking Oils: Choose olive oil, avocado oil, or canola oil for cooking.
   - Add Nuts and Seeds: Include unsalted nuts and seeds for healthy fats and crunch.

7. **Be Cautious with Processed Foods**:
   - Limit Processed Foods: Processed and packaged foods frequently have extra sugars, salt, and harmful fats.
   - Check for Hidden Sugars: Be wary of additional sugars in supposedly healthful items.

8. **Include a Variety of Colors**:
   - Diverse Fruits and Vegetables: Aim for a colorful array to guarantee a wide range of nutrients.
   - Seasonal Produce: Choose seasonal fruits and vegetables for freshness and possible cost savings.

9. **Choose Low-Sodium Options**:
   - Low-Sodium Broths and Canned Goods: Opt for low-sodium alternatives to control salt consumption.
   - Use Fresh or frozen veggies: If considering canned veggies, pick ones without extra salt.

10. **Mindful Snacking**:
    - Healthy Snack Options: Choose snacks like almonds, seeds, fresh fruit, or yogurt for balanced nutrients.
    - Portion Control: Pre-portion snacks to prevent overeating.

11. **Hydration is Key**:
    - Water is the Best Choice: Drink water during your shopping excursion and pick it as your main beverage.
    - Limit Sugary Drinks: Avoid sugary sodas and fruit drinks.

12. **Consider Diabetic-Friendly Substitutes**:
    - Sugar Alternatives: Explore non-nutritive sweeteners like stevia, monk fruit, or erythritol.
    - Whole Grain Alternatives: Look for whole grain or almond flour as alternatives in baking.

13. **Check for Sales and Discounts**:
    - Be Budget-Conscious: Look for promotions and discounts on diabetic-friendly meals without sacrificing on nutritional quality.

14. **Frozen Produce for Convenience**:
    - Frozen Fruits and Vegetables: Stock up on frozen choices for convenience and to avoid waste.

15. **Bring a Reusable Bag**:
    - Eco-Friendly Choices: Bring a reusable bag for a greener shopping experience.

16. **Stay Informed**:
    - Stay Updated on dietary: Keep yourself updated on dietary trends, particularly those related to diabetes treatment.

17. **Shop Online**:
    - Consider Online Shopping: Explore online food shopping for increased convenience, particularly if mobility is an issue.

By implementing these shopping recommendations into your routine, you may make healthier choices and better control your blood sugar levels while enjoying a range of tasty and healthy items. If in doubt, consider talking with a qualified nutritionist or healthcare expert for tailored counsel.

DELICIOUS BREAKFAST

Greek Yogurt Parfait

Prep Time: 5 minutes | **Cooking Time**: 0 minutes | **Total Time**: 5 minutes | **Servings**: 1

Ingredients:
- 1 cup plain, unsweetened Greek yogurt
- 1/2 cup mixed berries (fresh or frozen)
- 1/4 cup unsweetened granola or chopped nuts
- 1 tablespoon chia seeds
- 1/4 teaspoon ground cinnamon
- Optional: Stevia, honey, or maple syrup to taste (use sparingly)
- Optional: Fresh mint or basil for garnish

Directions:
1. Assemble the parfait: In a glass or container, layer 1/3 of the Greek yogurt. Top with 1/4 of the berries. Sprinkle with 1/3 of the granola and 1/2 tablespoon of chia seeds. Repeat with two more layers.
2. Sweeten as desired: Drizzle with a small amount of stevia, honey, or maple syrup, if using. Taste and adjust sweetness as needed.
3. Spice it up: Sprinkle with cinnamon and garnish with fresh mint or basil, if desired.
4. Serve immediately or refrigerate for up to 4 hours.

Nutritional Information: Calories: 300, Carbohydrates: 25g, Fiber: 8g, Protein: 20g, Fat: 8g, Sugar: 8g

Tips:
- Use unsweetened or lightly sweetened Greek yogurt to control sugar intake.
- Choose low-sugar or sugar-free granola or nuts to keep the carb count down.
- Opt for berries with a lower glycemic index, such as raspberries, blueberries, and strawberries.
- Add a scoop of low-sugar protein powder for an extra protein boost.
- Make it ahead of time: Assemble the parfait in a mason jar with a lid for a grab-and-go breakfast.
- Experiment with different flavors: Try mango, pineapple, or kiwi for a tropical twist. Top with a sprinkle of shredded coconut.
- Get creative: Drizzle with almond butter, peanut butter, or tahini for added flavor and healthy fats.

Oatmeal with Fresh Fruit

Prep Time: 5 minutes | **Cooking Time**: 5 minutes | **Total Time**: 10 minutes | **Serving Size**: 1

Ingredients:
- ½ cup rolled oats (old-fashioned or quick oats)
- 1 cup unsweetened plant-based milk (almond, soy, oat milk)
- ¼ cup water
- ¼ cup fresh berries (blueberries, raspberries, strawberries)
- ¼ cup chopped apple or pear
- 1 tablespoon chopped nuts or seeds (chia seeds, walnuts, almonds)
- ½ teaspoon ground cinnamon
- Pinch of salt (optional)
- Stevia or sugar-free sweetener to taste (optional)

Directions:
1. Prepare the oatmeal: In a saucepan, combine oats, milk, water, cinnamon, and salt (if using). Bring to a boil over medium heat, stirring occasionally. Reduce heat to low and simmer for 5 minutes, or until oats are cooked through and creamy.
2. While the oatmeal cooks, prepare the fruit: Wash and chop the berries and apple/pear.
3. Assemble the oatmeal: Divide the cooked oatmeal into a serving bowl. Top with fresh fruit, nuts/seeds, and a sprinkle of stevia or sweetener if desired. Enjoy warm!

Nutritional Information: Calories: 300, Carbohydrates: 40g, Fiber: 8g, Protein: 10g, Fat: 5g, Sugar: 15g

Tips:
- For added protein, stir in ¼ cup plain Greek yogurt before topping with fruit.
- Use unsweetened applesauce instead of sweetener for additional sweetness and moisture.
- Experiment with different spices like nutmeg, ginger, or cardamom for a flavor boost.
- Double the recipe for two servings.
- If you prefer colder oatmeal, prepare it the night before and refrigerate overnight. Reheat in the microwave for a quick and easy breakfast.
- For a heartier oatmeal, cook with quinoa or chia seeds for added protein and fiber.

Vegetable Omelette

Prep Time: 5 minutes | **Cooking Time**: 10 minutes | **Total Time**: 15 minutes | **Serving Size**: 1

Ingredients:
- 2 large eggs
- 1 tablespoon milk or unsweetened almond milk
- 1/4 cup chopped mixed vegetables (spinach, bell peppers, mushrooms, onions, etc.)
- 1/4 cup crumbled feta cheese or low-fat mozzarella cheese
- 1/4 teaspoon olive oil
- Salt and pepper to taste
- Optional: Chopped fresh herbs (parsley, basil, chives)

Directions:
1. Whisk together the eggs and milk in a bowl. Season with salt and pepper.
2. Heat olive oil in a non-stick pan over medium heat. Add the chopped vegetables and cook until softened, about 3-5 minutes.
3. Pour the egg mixture into the pan and tilt the pan to spread the eggs evenly. Let the eggs cook for about 30 seconds until the bottom starts to set.
4. Sprinkle the cheese over half of the omelette.
5. Using a spatula, fold the other half of the omelette over the cheese.
6. Continue cooking for another 2-3 minutes, or until the eggs are cooked through and the cheese is melted.
7. Slide the omelette onto a plate.
8. Garnish with fresh herbs, if desired.

Nutritional Information: Calories: 250, Protein: 18g, Carbohydrates: 8g, Fiber: 3g, Fat: 12g, Sodium: 200mg

Tips:
- For a lower-carb option, use cauliflower rice or shredded zucchini instead of other vegetables.
- Add a sprinkle of nutritional yeast for an extra boost of protein and B vitamins.
- Experiment with different spices and herbs to flavor your omelette.
- Serve your omelette with a side of whole-wheat toast or fruit for a more complete breakfast.

Whole Grain Toast with Avocado

Prep Time: 5 minutes | **Cooking Time**: 5 minutes | **Total Time**: 10 minutes | **Serving Size**: 1

Ingredients:
- 1 slice whole-grain bread (such as Ezekiel bread)
- 1/2 ripe avocado, mashed
- 1/4 teaspoon lemon juice
- Pinch of salt and pepper
- Optional toppings:
- 1 poached egg
- Sliced cherry tomatoes
- Chopped fresh herbs (such as cilantro or chives)
- A sprinkle of crumbled feta cheese
- Red pepper flakes

Directions:
1. Toast the bread to your desired level of doneness.
2. While the bread is toasting, mash the avocado in a bowl with the lemon juice, salt, and pepper.
3. Spread the mashed avocado on the toast.
4. If using, prepare your chosen toppings:
5. To poach an egg, bring a pot of water to a simmer. Crack the egg into a small bowl and gently slide it into the simmering water. Cook for 3-4 minutes, or until the whites are set and the yolk is runny. Remove with a slotted spoon.
6. Slice cherry tomatoes and crumble feta cheese (if using). Chop fresh herbs.
7. Top the avocado toast with your chosen toppings.

Nutritional Information: Calories: 240, Carbohydrates: 30g, Fiber: 8g, Protein: 6g, Fat: 14g

Tips:
- Use ripe avocados for the best flavor and texture.
- To prevent browning, add a squeeze of lemon juice to the mashed avocado.
- For a protein boost, add a poached egg, hard-boiled egg, or crumbled tofu.
- Get creative with your toppings! Experiment with different vegetables, herbs, and spices to find your favorite combinations.
- Consider portion sizes. This recipe makes one serving, but you can adjust the amount of bread and avocado based on your individual needs and calorie goals.

Cottage Cheese and Pineapple Bowl

Prep Time: 5 minutes | **Cooking Time**: N/A | **Total Time**: 5 minutes | **Serving Size**: 1

Ingredients:

- 1/2 cup (125g) plain, low-fat cottage cheese
- 1/2 cup (80g) fresh pineapple, chunks or diced
- 1/4 cup (60g) berries (your choice - blueberries, raspberries, strawberries)
- 1 tablespoon chopped nuts (walnuts, almonds, pecans)
- 1/4 teaspoon ground cinnamon
- 1 tablespoon unsweetened shredded coconut (optional)
- 1 tablespoon chia seeds (optional)
- 1/4 cup unsweetened almond milk (optional)

Directions:

1. In a bowl, combine the cottage cheese and pineapple. Gently mix until just combined.
2. Top with berries, nuts, cinnamon, and any other desired toppings.
3. If desired, drizzle with a small amount of unsweetened almond milk for added moisture.
4. Enjoy immediately

Nutritional Information: Calories: 200, Carbohydrates: 20g, Fiber: 3g, Net Carbs: 17g, Protein: 20g, Fat: 4g

Tips:

- For a sweeter bowl, sprinkle with a touch of stevia or monk fruit sweetener.
- Substitute the pineapple with other diabetic-friendly fruits like pears, apples, or grapefruit.
- Add a scoop of high-protein Greek yogurt for extra creaminess and protein.
- Use low-carb granola for a bit of crunch.
- Refrigerate leftovers for up to 2 days.

Chia Seed Pudding

Prep Time: 5 minutes | **Cooking Time**: 0 minutes | **Total Time**: 5 minutes | Serving Size: 1

Ingredients:

- 1/4 cup chia seeds
- 1 cup unsweetened almond milk (or other low-carb milk of your choice)
- 1/4 teaspoon vanilla extract
- 1/4 teaspoon ground cinnamon
- Pinch of stevia or monk fruit sweetener (optional)
- Toppings (optional): fresh berries, sliced nuts, unsweetened shredded coconut, chia seeds for extra crunch

Directions:

1. In a jar or container with a lid, combine chia seeds, almond milk, vanilla extract, cinnamon, and sweetener (if using). Stir well until everything is combined.
2. Cover the jar and refrigerate for at least 2 hours, or overnight. During this time, the chia seeds will absorb the liquid and thicken into a pudding-like consistency.
3. When ready to serve, stir the pudding again. Top with your desired toppings, such as fresh berries, nuts, coconut, or additional chia seeds.

Nutritional Information: Calories: 230 Carbohydrates: 12g, Fiber: 7g, Protein: 5g, Fat: 14g, Sugar: 3g

Tips:

- You can experiment with different flavors by adding spices like nutmeg, ginger, or cardamom.
- For a richer pudding, use half milk and half unsweetened yogurt.
- If you prefer a thinner pudding, add a little more milk after refrigeration.
- This pudding can be stored in the refrigerator for up to 3 days.

Quinoa Breakfast Bowl

Prep Time: 5 minutes | **Cooking Time**: 15 minutes | **Total Time**: 20 minutes | **Serving Size**: 1

Ingredients:
- 1/2 cup uncooked quinoa, rinsed
- 1 cup water or unsweetened almond milk
- 1/4 teaspoon ground cinnamon
- Pinch of salt
- 1/4 cup sliced berries (fresh or frozen)
- 1/4 cup chopped nuts (almonds, walnuts, pecans)
- 1 tablespoon chia seeds
- 1/4 cup plain Greek yogurt (optional)
- Stevia or sugar-free sweetener to taste (optional)

Directions:
1. Cook the quinoa: In a saucepan, combine rinsed quinoa, water/almond milk, cinnamon, and salt. Bring to a boil, then reduce heat, cover, and simmer for 15 minutes or until quinoa is fluffy and cooked through. Fluff with a fork and set aside to cool slightly.
2. Assemble the bowl: Divide the cooked quinoa into a serving bowl. Top with berries, nuts, and chia seeds.
3. Add extra protein and creaminess (optional): Dollop some plain Greek yogurt on top for added protein and creaminess.
4. Sweeten to taste (optional): If desired, drizzle with a small amount of stevia or sugar-free sweetener for added sweetness.

Nutritional Information: Calories: 350, Carbohydrates: 40g, Fiber: 13g, Protein: 12g, Fat: 8g, Sodium: 150mg

Tips:
- To save time, cook a larger batch of quinoa ahead of time and store it in the refrigerator for up to 5 days.
- Get creative with your toppings! You can use different types of fruits, nuts, seeds, and spices to customize your bowl.
- For a savory option, replace the berries with chopped vegetables like roasted bell peppers, avocado, or spinach.
- If you don't have Greek yogurt, you can use unsweetened almond milk or mashed avocado for a creamier texture.

Smoothie Bowl

Prep Time: 5 minutes | **Cooking Time**: None | **Total Time**: 5 minutes | **Serving Size**: 1 bowl

Ingredients:
- 1/2 cup unsweetened almond milk
- 1/4 cup unsweetened shredded coconut
- 1/4 cup frozen mango chunks
- 1/4 cup frozen pineapple chunks
- 1/4 cup fresh or frozen spinach
- 1/4 cup plain Greek yogurt
- 1 scoop unflavored protein powder (optional)
- 1/4 teaspoon ground cinnamon
- 1/4 teaspoon ground ginger
- 1/4 cup fresh berries (optional)
- 1/4 cup chopped nuts and seeds (optional)

Directions:
1. Combine all ingredients except toppings in a blender and blend until smooth and creamy. You may need to add more almond milk if the mixture is too thick.
2. Pour the smoothie mixture into a bowl.
3. Top with your favorite toppings, such as fresh berries, chopped nuts and seeds, unsweetened coconut flakes, or a drizzle of chia seeds.

Nutritional Information: Calories: 350, Carbohydrates: 35g, Fiber: 8g, Sugar: 15g, Protein: 15g, Fat: 10g

Tips:
- For a thicker smoothie bowl, use frozen fruit instead of fresh.
- You can add a tablespoon of chia seeds or flaxseed meal to the smoothie for extra fiber and healthy fats.
- If you don't have protein powder, you can use an extra scoop of Greek yogurt or 1/4 cup of cottage cheese.
- Taste the smoothie before adding any sweetener. You may find that the natural sweetness of the fruit is enough. If you do want to add sweetener, use a small amount of stevia or monk fruit extract.
- Be sure to check the nutrition labels of all ingredients, especially if you are following a specific carbohydrate or calorie target.

Egg and Vegetable Wrap

Prep Time: 5 minutes | **Cooking Time**: 10 minutes | **Total Time**: 15 minutes | **Serving Size**: 1

Ingredients:
- 1 whole wheat tortilla (8-inch)
- 1 large egg
- 1 egg white
- 1/4 cup chopped spinach
- 1/4 cup chopped bell pepper
- 1/4 cup chopped mushrooms
- 1/4 cup shredded reduced-fat cheddar cheese
- 1 tablespoon salsa
- 1/4 avocado, sliced (optional)
- Salt and pepper to taste

Directions:
1. Prep the vegetables: Wash and chop the spinach, bell pepper, and mushrooms.
2. Cook the eggs: In a non-stick pan, heat a spray of cooking oil over medium heat. Scramble the egg and egg white until cooked through. Season with salt and pepper.
3. Assemble the wrap: Spread the warm scrambled egg mixture onto the tortilla. Top with spinach, bell pepper, mushrooms, cheese, salsa, and avocado (if using).
4. Roll and enjoy: Fold the bottom of the tortilla up over the filling, then fold the sides in. Roll up tightly and enjoy

Nutritional Information: Calories: 300, Carbohydrates: 20g, Fiber: 5g, Protein: 20g, Fat: 10g

Tips:
1. For a lower-carb option, use a low-carb tortilla or lettuce wrap.
2. Add other vegetables of your choice, such as onions, tomatoes, or zucchini.
3. Use a different type of cheese, such as feta or mozzarella.
4. Add a dollop of Greek yogurt for extra protein and creaminess.
5. Toast the tortilla for a crispy wrap.
6. Prepare the vegetables and cheese the night before for even quicker assembly in the morning.

Sweet Potato Hash

Prep Time: 10 minutes | **Cooking Time**: 20 minutes | **Total Time**: 30 minutes | **Serving Size**: 2

Ingredients:
- 1 medium sweet potato, peeled and diced
- 1/2 onion, diced
- 1 bell pepper (any color), diced
- 1/2 cup mushrooms, sliced
- 1 clove garlic, minced
- 1/2 teaspoon ground cumin
- 1/4 teaspoon chili powder
- Pinch of cinnamon
- Pinch of cayenne pepper (optional)
- 1/4 cup chopped fresh cilantro
- 2 tablespoons olive oil
- 2 eggs (optional)
- Salt and pepper to taste

Directions:
1. Prep the vegetables: Peel and dice the sweet potato, onion, bell pepper, and mushrooms. Mince the garlic. Chop the cilantro.
2. Cook the sweet potato: Heat olive oil in a large skillet over medium heat. Add the sweet potato and cook for 10 minutes, stirring occasionally, until softened.
3. Add remaining vegetables: Add the onion, bell pepper, and mushrooms to the pan. Cook for 5 minutes, stirring occasionally, until softened.
4. Season and spice: Add the garlic, cumin, chili powder, cinnamon, and cayenne pepper (if using). Cook for 1 minute, stirring constantly, to release the flavors.
5. Scramble the eggs (optional): If using eggs, push the vegetables to one side of the pan and crack the eggs into the empty space. Scramble the eggs until cooked through, then stir them into the vegetables.
6. Finish and serve: Season with salt and pepper to taste. Garnish with chopped cilantro and serve immediately.

Nutritional Information: Calories: 350, Carbohydrates: 40g, Fiber: 8g, Protein: 10g, Fat: 10g, Sodium: 300mg

Tips:
- For a vegan option, omit the eggs and use a tablespoon of chia seeds mixed with 3 tablespoons of water for an "egg-like" texture.
- Add other vegetables you like, such as spinach, kale, or zucchini.
- Top your hash with a dollop of Greek yogurt, cottage cheese, or avocado for added protein and healthy fats.
- Serve with a whole-wheat toast or wrap for a complete breakfast.
- Adjust the spices to your liking.
- If you have cooked sweet potato on hand, simply dice it and add it to the pan with the other vegetables.

Whole Wheat Pancakes with Berries

Prep Time: 10 minutes | **Cooking Time**: 15-20 minutes | **Total Time**: 25-30 minutes
Servings: 2

Ingredients:
- 1 cup whole wheat flour
- 1 teaspoon baking powder
- 1/2 teaspoon baking soda
- 1/4 teaspoon salt
- 1 tablespoon granulated sweetener of your choice (optional, such as stevia, erythritol, or monk fruit sweetener)
- 1 large egg
- 1 cup unsweetened almond milk (or other milk of your choice)
- 1 tablespoon melted coconut oil (or other cooking oil)
- 1/2 cup fresh mixed berries (such as blueberries, raspberries, strawberries)
- Greek yogurt or whipped cream (optional, for topping)

Directions:
1. Prepare the dry ingredients: In a large bowl, whisk together the flour, baking powder, baking soda, salt, and sweetener (if using).
2. Mix the wet ingredients: In a separate bowl, whisk together the egg and milk. Gently whisk the wet ingredients into the dry ingredients until just combined. Do not overmix, as this will make the pancakes tough.
3. Heat the pan: Preheat a lightly greased griddle or non-stick pan over medium heat.
4. Cook the pancakes: Pour 1/4 cup of batter onto the pan for each pancake. Cook for 2-3 minutes per side, or until golden brown and bubbles appear on the surface.
5. Assemble and serve: Top each pancake with fresh berries and a dollop of Greek yogurt or whipped cream (optional). Enjoy immediately

Nutritional Information: Calories: 250, Carbohydrates: 35g, Fiber: 5g, Protein: 8g, Fat: 6g, Sugar

Tips:
- For extra fiber and protein, add 1/4 cup ground flaxseed or chia seeds to the dry ingredients.
- If the batter seems too thick, add a tablespoon of milk at a time until it reaches a desired consistency.
- You can use various sweeteners depending on your preference. Remember to adjust the amount based on the sweetness of your chosen sweetener.
- For a richer flavor, use buttermilk instead of almond milk.
- Experiment with different types of berries or top with sliced banana, nuts, or seeds for additional flavor and nutrients.
- This recipe is easily doubled or tripled to feed more people.
- Leftover pancakes can be stored in an airtight container in the refrigerator for up to 3 days. Reheat in a toaster or microwave before serving.

Salmon and Cream Cheese Bagel

Prep Time: 5 minutes | **Cooking Time**: 5 minutes | **Total Time**: 10 minutes | **Serving Size**: 1

Ingredients:

- 1 whole-wheat bagel, sliced and toasted
- 2 tablespoons reduced-fat cream cheese
- 2 ounces smoked salmon, thinly sliced
- ¼ cup chopped vegetables (cucumber, tomato, red onion, optional)
- ¼ teaspoon fresh dill, chopped (optional)
- ¼ teaspoon lemon juice (optional)
- Pinch of black pepper

Directions:

1. Toast the bagel: Slice the bagel in half and toast to desired level of crispness. While toasting, prepare the other ingredients.
2. Prepare the cream cheese: In a small bowl, mix the reduced-fat cream cheese with dill and lemon juice (optional). Adjust seasonings to taste.
3. Assemble the bagel: Spread the flavored cream cheese evenly on one half of the toasted bagel.
4. Layer the toppings: Arrange the smoked salmon slices on top of the cream cheese. Add chopped vegetables for extra flavor and fiber (optional).
5. Season and serve: Sprinkle with black pepper and serve immediately.

Nutritional Information: Calories: 350, Carbohydrates: 40g, Net carbs: 25g, Protein: 20g, Fat: 15g, Fiber: 5g, Sodium: 300mg

Tips:

- Choose whole-wheat bagels for higher fiber content, which helps regulate blood sugar.
- Opt for reduced-fat cream cheese to lower fat and calorie intake.
- Use low-sodium cream cheese to manage sodium intake.
- Be mindful of portion sizes and choose lean protein sources like smoked salmon.
- Add vegetables for additional nutrients and fiber.
- Monitor your blood sugar levels after consuming this breakfast.

Almond Flour Waffles

Prep Time: 5 minutes **Cooking Time**: 5-7 minutes | **Total Time**: 10-12 minutes | **Serving Size**: 2

Ingredients:
- 1 cup almond flour
- 1/4 teaspoon baking powder
- 1/4 teaspoon baking soda
- 1/4 teaspoon salt
- 1 egg
- 1/4 cup unsweetened almond milk
- 1 tablespoon melted butter or coconut oil
- 1 teaspoon vanilla extract
- Optional: 1/4 teaspoon ground cinnamon, sweetener of your choice (stevia, erythritol

Directions:
1. Whisk dry ingredients: In a large bowl, whisk together almond flour, baking powder, baking soda, and salt.
2. Combine wet ingredients: In a separate bowl, whisk together the egg, almond milk, melted butter/coconut oil, vanilla extract, and optional sweetener and cinnamon.
3. Combine wet and dry ingredients: Pour the wet ingredients into the dry ingredients and mix until just combined. Be careful not to overmix, as this can make the waffles tough.
4. Preheat waffle iron: Preheat your waffle iron according to the manufacturer's instructions. Lightly grease the waffle iron if needed.
5. Cook waffles: Pour the batter evenly onto the waffle iron and cook for 5-7 minutes, or until golden brown and crispy.
6. Serve: Serve your waffles immediately with your favorite low-carb toppings, such as berries, whipped cream made with sugar substitute, chopped nuts, or a drizzle of low-sugar syrup.

Nutritional Information: Calories: 300, Carbohydrates: 6g, Fiber: 3g, Protein: 10g, Fat: 20g

Tips:
- If the batter seems too thick, add a little more almond milk, 1 tablespoon at a time, until it reaches a desired consistency.
- You can adjust the amount of sweetener to your taste.
- For added protein, you can add a scoop of your favorite protein powder to the batter.
- You can store leftover waffles in an airtight container in the refrigerator for up to 3 days. Reheat them in a toaster or microwave before serving.
- Additional Notes:
- It's important to consult with your doctor or registered dietitian before making any major changes to your diet, especially if you have diabetes. They can help you create a personalized meal plan that meets your individual needs and goals.
- Be sure to monitor your blood sugar levels after eating these waffles to see how they affect you.

Veggie Breakfast Burrito

Prep Time: 10 minutes | **Cooking Time**: 15 minutes | **Total Time**: 25 minutes | **Serving Size**: 1 burrito

Ingredients:
- 1 whole-wheat tortilla
- 1/2 cup scrambled eggs (made with 1 egg and a splash of milk)
- 1/4 cup black beans, rinsed and drained
- 1/4 cup chopped bell pepper (any color)
- 1/4 cup chopped mushrooms
- 1/4 cup chopped spinach
- 1/4 cup shredded low-fat cheese
- 1/4 avocado, mashed
- 1 tablespoon salsa (optional)
- Salt and pepper to taste

Directions:
1. Prepare the eggs: Scramble the egg in a pan with a splash of milk and season with salt and pepper. Set aside.
2. Saute the vegetables: Heat a pan over medium heat and add a drizzle of olive oil. Saute the bell pepper and mushrooms until softened, about 5 minutes. Add the spinach and cook until wilted.
3. Assemble the burrito: Warm the tortilla in a dry pan or microwave. Spread mashed avocado on half of the tortilla. Layer the scrambled eggs, black beans, sauteed vegetables, and cheese on top.
4. Roll and enjoy: Fold the bottom of the tortilla up over the filling, then fold in the sides. Roll the burrito tightly and enjoy immediately.
5. Optional variations:
6. Add a dollop of low-fat Greek yogurt for extra protein and creaminess.
7. Use a whole-wheat tortilla wrap for added fiber.
8. Add a sprinkle of your favorite herbs or spices for additional flavor.
9. Top with a dollop of hot sauce for a spicy kick.

Nutritional Information: Calories: 350, Carbohydrates: 30g, Fiber: 5g, Protein: 20g, Fat: 10g, Saturated fat 2g, Sodium: 300mg

Tips:
- To save time, scramble the eggs and saute the vegetables the night before.
- Wrap the burritos in foil and store them in the refrigerator for up to 3 days. Reheat in the microwave or oven before serving.
- Feel free to adjust the ingredients to your preferences and dietary needs.

Muesli with Yogurt

Prep Time: 5 minutes | **Cooking Time**: 0 minutes | **Total Time**: 5 minutes | **Serving Size**: 1

Ingredients:

- 1/2 cup rolled oats (not quick oats)
- 1/2 cup unsweetened plain Greek yogurt
- 1/4 cup unsweetened almond milk
- 1/4 cup mixed berries (fresh or frozen)
- 1/4 cup chopped nuts (almonds, walnuts, pecans)
- 1 tablespoon ground flaxseed
- 1/2 teaspoon cinnamon
- Optional: 1/4 teaspoon stevia extract (for additional sweetness)

Directions:

1. Soak the oats: The night before, combine the rolled oats and almond milk in a bowl or container. Cover and refrigerate overnight.
2. Assemble the bowl: In the morning, stir in the Greek yogurt, berries, nuts, flaxseed, and cinnamon.
3. Sweeten to taste: If desired, stir in the stevia extract for additional sweetness.

Nutritional Information: Calories: 350, Carbohydrates: 35g, Fiber: 10g, Protein: 15g, Fat: 10g

Tips:

- You can use different types of nuts and seeds in this recipe.
- Add a sprinkle of unsweetened shredded coconut for extra texture and flavor.
- If you don't have time to soak the oats overnight, you can microwave them for 1-2 minutes with a small amount of water or milk.
- Be sure to choose unsweetened or low-sugar yogurt and toppings to keep the carbohydrate content in check.
- Talk to your doctor or registered dietitian for personalized advice on managing your diabetes with diet.

Egg Muffins

Prep Time: 10 minutes | **Cooking Time**: 20-25 minutes | **Total Time**: 30-35 minutes
Servings: 6 muffins

Ingredients:

- 6 eggs
- 1/4 cup unsweetened almond milk or skim milk
- 1/4 cup chopped vegetables (such as spinach, bell peppers, onions)
- 1/4 cup shredded cheese (such as cheddar, Swiss, or mozzarella)
- 1/4 teaspoon dried herbs (such as oregano, basil, or thyme)
- Salt and pepper to taste
- Optional Add-ins:
- 1/4 cup cooked turkey bacon or sausage
- 1/4 cup chopped sun-dried tomatoes
- 1/4 cup crumbled feta cheese
- 1/4 cup cooked black beans

Directions:

1. Preheat oven to 350°F (175°C). Grease a 6-cup muffin tin with cooking spray.
2. In a large bowl, whisk together eggs and milk. Stir in vegetables, cheese, herbs, salt, and pepper.
3. Divide the egg mixture evenly among the prepared muffin cups.
4. Add any optional add-ins you like.
5. Bake for 20-25 minutes, or until the eggs are set and the centers are no longer runny.
6. Let cool slightly before serving.

Nutritional Information: Calories: 150-200, Carbohydrates: 3-5g, Protein: 12-15g, Fat: 10-15g, Sodium: 200-250mg

Tips:

- For a heartier muffin, add 1-2 tablespoons of cooked quinoa or brown rice to each cup.
- To make ahead of time, bake the egg muffins and store them in an airtight container in the refrigerator for up to 3 days. Reheat in the microwave or oven before serving.
- Get creative with your add-ins! There are endless possibilities.
- Be sure to check the nutrition labels of any additional ingredients you use to ensure they fit within your diabetes meal plan.

Peanut Butter and Banana Sandwich

Prep Time: 5 minutes | **Cooking Time**: 0 minutes | **Total Time**: 5 minutes | **Serving Size**: 1 sandwich

Ingredients:

- 2 slices whole-wheat bread
- 2 tablespoons natural peanut butter (without added sugar)
- 1/2 medium banana, sliced
- 1/4 teaspoon ground cinnamon (optional)
- Pinch of salt (optional)

Directions:

1. Toast the bread (optional): If desired, toast the bread slices lightly in a toaster oven or pan.
2. Spread the peanut butter: Spread 1 tablespoon of peanut butter on each slice of bread.
3. Prepare the banana: Slice the banana into thin rounds.
4. Assemble the sandwich: Place the banana slices on one slice of bread. Sprinkle with cinnamon and salt (optional). Top with the second slice of bread, peanut butter side down.
5. Enjoy immediately: This sandwich is best enjoyed fresh.

Nutritional Information: Calories: 300, Carbohydrates: 35g, Protein: 10g, Fat: 12g, Fiber: 3g, Sodium: 180mg

Tips:

- For a more filling sandwich, use thicker slices of bread or add another tablespoon of peanut butter.
- To make this sandwich vegan, use sunflower seed butter instead of peanut butter.
- If you have a ripe banana, you can mash it instead of slicing it for a creamier texture.
- You can add other toppings to your sandwich, such as sliced strawberries, blueberries, or a sprinkle of chia seeds.
- If you're monitoring your sodium intake, be mindful of the amount of salt you add.

Coconut Flour Porridge

Prep Time: 5 minutes | **Cooking Time**: 5-7 minutes | **Total Time**: 10-12 minutes | **Serving Size**: 1

Ingredients:

- 2 tablespoons coconut flour
- 1/2 cup unsweetened almond milk or other low-carb milk
- 1/4 cup water
- 1/4 teaspoon ground cinnamon
- Pinch of salt
- 1/4 teaspoon chia seeds (optional)
- Optional toppings: Berries, chopped nuts, unsweetened shredded coconut, low-carb sweetener

Directions:

1. In a small saucepan, whisk together the coconut flour, almond milk, water, cinnamon, and salt.
2. Heat over medium heat, stirring constantly, until the mixture thickens and begins to simmer. This will take about 3-5 minutes.
3. If desired, stir in the chia seeds and cook for an additional minute.
4. Remove from heat and pour into a bowl.
5. Top with your favorite low-carb and diabetes-friendly toppings.

Nutritional Information: Calories: 250, Carbohydrates: 10g, Net carbs: 5g, Fiber: 8g, Protein: 8g, Fat: 15g

Tips:

- For a creamier porridge, add a tablespoon of unsweetened nut butter or coconut butter before serving.
- You can also add a scoop of protein powder for an extra boost of protein.
- To make this porridge ahead of time, simply prepare it as directed and store it in an airtight container in the refrigerator for up to 3 days. Reheat gently before serving.
- Be sure to adjust the amount of sweetener to your taste preference.
- It's important to monitor your blood sugar levels after consuming this dish, as individual responses may vary.

Avocado and Tomato Toast

Prep Time: 5 minutes | **Cooking Time**: 0 minutes | **Total Time**: 5 minutes | **Serving Size**: 1 toast

Ingredients:

- 1 slice whole-wheat or rye bread
- 1/4 avocado, mashed
- 1 medium tomato, sliced
- 1/4 cup crumbled feta cheese (optional)
- 1 tablespoon fresh herbs (e.g., basil, parsley, chives)
- 1/4 teaspoon balsamic glaze (optional)
- Salt and pepper to taste

Directions:

1. Toast the bread: Toast your bread to your desired level of crispness.
2. Mash the avocado: In a small bowl, mash the avocado with a fork. Add a squeeze of lemon juice or lime juice to prevent browning (optional). Season with salt and pepper.
3. Assemble the toast: Spread the mashed avocado onto the toasted bread.
4. Add toppings: Layer the sliced tomato on top of the avocado.
5. Optional additions: Add crumbled feta cheese for extra protein and creaminess. Sprinkle with fresh herbs for flavor and brightness. Drizzle with balsamic glaze for a touch of sweetness and acidity.

Nutritional Information: Calories: 240, Carbohydrates: 22g, Fiber: 8g, Net Carbs: 14g, Protein: 5g, Fat: 16g

Tips:

- Use ripe but firm avocados for the best texture.
- Choose low-sodium feta cheese to keep the sodium content in check.
- For a warm twist, briefly toast the sliced tomatoes in a pan with a drizzle of olive oil before adding them to the toast.
- For extra protein, add a poached or fried egg on top.
- Experiment with different herbs and spices to personalize your toast.

Berry and Spinach Smoothie

Prep Time: 5 minutes | **Cooking Time**: N/A | **Total Time**: 5 minutes | **Serving Size**: 1 person

Ingredients:

- 1 cup mixed berries (fresh or frozen)
- 1/2 cup baby spinach
- 1/2 banana (frozen or fresh)
- 1/2 cup unsweetened almond milk (or other plant-based milk)
- 1/4 cup plain Greek yogurt (optional, for added protein)
- 1 scoop protein powder (optional, for added protein and satiety)
- 1/4 teaspoon ground cinnamon (optional, for flavor)
- Ice cubes (optional, for desired consistency)

Directions:

1. Gather your ingredients. Make sure the banana is peeled and chopped if using fresh.
2. Combine all ingredients in a blender and blend until smooth. Adjust the consistency by adding more milk or ice cubes if needed.
3. Pour into a glass and enjoy

Nutritional Information: Calories: 250, Carbohydrates: 30g, Fiber: 5g, Protein: 8g, Fat: 4g, Sugar: 15g, Vitamin C: 50% DV, Vitamin K: 100% DV

Tips:

- Use a variety of berries for different flavors and nutritional benefits.
- If using frozen fruit, you may not need ice cubes.
- Add a teaspoon of chia seeds for extra fiber and omega-3 fatty acids.
- Adjust the sweetness to your preference. You can use a natural sweetener like stevia if desired.
- For a thicker smoothie, use less milk or add a scoop of nut butter.
- If you don't have Greek yogurt, you can use cottage cheese or tofu for added protein.
- Feel free to customize this recipe with other fruits and vegetables you enjoy

WHOLESOME LUNCH

Grilled Chicken Salad

Prep Time: 10 minutes **Cooking Time**: 20 minutes | **Total Time**: 30 minutes **Serving Size**: 1

Ingredients:
- 4 oz. boneless, skinless chicken breast
- 1 tbsp. olive oil
- 1/2 tsp. dried oregano
- 1/4 tsp. garlic powder
- 1/4 tsp. black pepper
- 2 cups mixed greens
- 1/2 cup cherry tomatoes, halved
- 1/4 cup cucumber, diced
- 1/4 cup red onion, thinly sliced
- 1/4 cup crumbled feta cheese (optional)
- 1/4 avocado, sliced (optional)

Dressing:
- 2 tbsps. olive oil
- 1 tbsps. lemon juice
- 1 tsp. Dijon mustard
- 1/2 tsp. dried oregano
- 1/4 tsp. garlic powder
- Pinch of salt and pepper

Directions:
1. Marinate the chicken: In a small bowl, combine olive oil, oregano, garlic powder, and black pepper. Rub the mixture on the chicken breast and marinate for at least 10 minutes.
2. Grill the chicken: Preheat your grill to medium-high heat. Grill the chicken breast for 5-7 minutes per side, or until cooked through. Let the chicken cool slightly, then chop or shred it into bite-sized pieces.
3. Assemble the salad: In a large bowl, combine the mixed greens, cherry tomatoes, cucumber, red onion, and feta cheese (if using).
4. Make the dressing: In a small bowl, whisk together olive oil, lemon juice, Dijon mustard, oregano, garlic powder, salt, and pepper.
5. Top the salad: Add the chopped chicken to the salad and drizzle with the dressing. Garnish with avocado slices (if using).

Nutritional Information: Calories: 350, Carbohydrates: 15g, Fiber: 5g, Protein: 30g
Fat: 15g, Healthy fats: 5g, Sodium: 300mg

Tips:
- Use boneless, skinless chicken thighs for a more flavorful salad.
- Add other vegetables to the salad, such as bell peppers, carrots, or celery.
- Use a low-fat yogurt-based dressing if you prefer a lighter option.
- Be sure to check the nutrition labels of all ingredients, especially the dressing, to ensure they fit your individual needs.
- Adjust the amount of dressing to your preference.

Quinoa and Black Bean Bowl

Prep Time: 10 minutes | **Cooking Time**: 15 minutes | **Total Time**: 25 minutes | **Servings**: 2

Ingredients:
- 1 cup dry quinoa, rinsed
- 1 ½ cups vegetable broth
- 1 can (15 oz) black beans, rinsed and drained
- 1 cup mixed greens
- ½ cup cherry tomatoes, halved
- ½ cucumber, diced
- ¼ red onion, thinly sliced
- 1 avocado, diced
- ¼ cup crumbled feta cheese (optional)
- ¼ cup chopped fresh cilantro
- Lime wedges, for squeezing
- Olive oil
- Apple cider vinegar
- Dried oregano
- Garlic powder
- Salt and pepper

Directions:
1. Cook the quinoa: In a saucepan, combine rinsed quinoa and vegetable broth. Bring to a boil, then reduce heat, cover, and simmer for 15 minutes or until fluffy. Fluff with a fork and set aside to cool slightly.
2. Assemble the bowls: Divide mixed greens, black beans, tomatoes, cucumber, red onion, and avocado between two bowls.
3. Top with cooked quinoa: Top each bowl with the cooled quinoa.
4. Make the dressing: In a small bowl, whisk together olive oil, apple cider vinegar, oregano, garlic powder, salt, and pepper to taste.
5. Drizzle and garnish: Drizzle each bowl with the dressing and top with crumbled feta cheese (optional) and fresh cilantro. Serve with lime wedges for squeezing.

Nutritional Information: Calories: 400, Carbohydrates: 40g, Fiber: 10g, Protein: 20g, Fat: 10g, Sodium: 300mg

Tips:
- To save time, use pre-cooked quinoa.
- Adjust the toppings to your liking. Other options include corn, bell peppers, chopped spinach, or salsa.
- Control sodium intake by using low-sodium black beans and feta cheese (or omitting it).
- Feel free to adjust the dressing amounts to your taste preference.
- This recipe is easily doubled or tripled for meal prep.
- For added protein, consider grilling some chicken or shrimp to add to the bowl.

Salmon and Vegetable Stir-Fry

Prep Time: 10 minutes | **Cooking Time**: 15 minutes | **Total Time**: 25 minutes | **Serving Size**: 2

Ingredients:
- 1 tablespoon avocado oil or canola oil
- 1 small onion, thinly sliced
- 1 bell pepper, sliced
- 1 cup broccoli florets
- 1 cup snow peas or sugar snap peas
- 4 ounces skinless, boneless salmon fillet, cut into bite-sized pieces
- 1/4 cup low-sodium soy sauce
- 1 tablespoon rice vinegar
- 1 tablespoon brown sugar (or substitute with a sugar-free sweetener)
- 1 tablespoon cornstarch
- 1/4 cup water
- 1/4 teaspoon ground ginger
- 1/4 teaspoon garlic powder
- Chopped fresh cilantro, for garnish (optional)
- Cooked brown rice or quinoa, for serving

Directions:
1. Prepare the vegetables: Wash and chop the onion, bell pepper, broccoli florets, and snow peas.
2. Marinate the salmon: In a small bowl, combine the soy sauce, rice vinegar, brown sugar (or sweetener), cornstarch, water, ginger, and garlic powder. Whisk well to dissolve the cornstarch. Add the salmon pieces and marinate for 5 minutes.
3. Heat the oil: Heat the oil in a large skillet or wok over medium-high heat.
4. Stir-fry the vegetables: Add the onion and bell pepper to the pan and cook for 2-3 minutes, until softened. Add the broccoli and snow peas and cook for another 2-3 minutes, until crisp-tender. Remove the vegetables from the pan and set aside.
5. Cook the salmon: Add the marinated salmon to the pan and cook for 3-4 minutes per side, or until cooked through.
6. Thicken the sauce: Add the sauce mixture to the pan and bring to a simmer. Cook for 1-2 minutes, stirring constantly, until the sauce thickens slightly.
7. Combine everything: Return the vegetables to the pan with the salmon and sauce. Toss to coat everything evenly.
8. Serve: Serve immediately over cooked brown rice or quinoa. Garnish with chopped fresh cilantro, if desired.

Nutritional Information: Calories: 400, Carbohydrates: 20g, Fiber: 5g, Protein: 30g, Fat: 15g (including healthy omega-3 fats Sodium: 300mg

Tips:
You can use other types of fish, such as cod or halibut, instead of salmon.
For a spicier stir-fry, add a pinch of red pepper flakes to the sauce.
To make the stir-fry even more diabetes-friendly, use brown rice or quinoa instead of white rice. You can also use cauliflower rice for a low-carb option.
Adjust the amount of sodium in the soy sauce to fit your individual needs.
Feel free to add other vegetables to the stir-fry, such as carrots, snap peas, or mushrooms.
For extra flavor, you can marinate the salmon in a teriyaki sauce or a mixture of olive oil, lemon juice, and herbs.

Turkey and Hummus Wrap

Prep Time: 5 minutes | **Cooking Time**: None | **Total Time**: 5 minutes | **Serving Size**: 1 wrap

Ingredients:

- 1 whole wheat tortilla (9-inch)
- 3 tablespoons hummus (choose a low-fat option if desired)
- 4 ounces sliced lean turkey breast
- 1/2 cup baby spinach
- 1/4 cup shredded cucumber
- 1/4 cup sliced red bell pepper
- 1/4 cup crumbled feta cheese (optional)
- 1 tablespoon fresh lemon juice
- Salt and pepper to taste

Directions:

1. Spread hummus evenly over the entire tortilla.
2. Layer turkey, spinach, cucumber, and red bell pepper on top of the hummus.
3. Crumble feta cheese over the top, if using.
4. Drizzle with lemon juice and season with salt and pepper to taste.
5. Carefully roll up the tortilla, starting from one end and tucking in the sides as you go.
6. Cut the wrap in half and enjoy

Nutritional Information: Calories: 350, Carbohydrates: 25g, Protein: 30g, Fat: 10g, Fiber: 5g, Sodium: 300mg

Tips:

- Use a low-carb tortilla to further reduce the carbohydrate content.
- Add other vegetables like shredded carrots, lettuce, or tomatoes.
- Swap the feta cheese for another low-fat option like goat cheese or mozzarella.
- Use roasted turkey breast for a smoky flavor.
- Drizzle with a low-sugar vinaigrette instead of lemon juice for added flavor.
- Pack in a cooler with an ice pack if you're taking it for lunch on the go.

Mediterranean Chickpea Salad

Prep Time: 15 minutes | **Cooking Time**: 0 minutes | **Total Time**: 15 minutes | **Servings**: 2

Ingredients:
- 1 (15oz) can chickpeas, drained and rinsed
- 1/2 cup diced cucumber
- 1/2 cup diced red bell pepper
- 1/4 cup diced red onion
- 1/4 cup crumbled feta cheese (replace with low-fat if desired)
- 1/4 cup chopped fresh parsley
- 2 tablespoons extra virgin olive oil
- 1 tablespoon lemon juice
- 1/2 teaspoon dried oregano
- 1/4 teaspoon garlic powder
- Salt and black pepper to taste
- Optional Additions:
- 1/4 cup cherry tomatoes, halved
- 1/4 cup Kalamata olives, sliced
- 1/2 avocado, diced
- 1/4 cup crumbled fresh mint

Directions:
1. Prep your ingredients: Dice the cucumber, bell pepper, and red onion. Crumble the feta cheese and chop the parsley.
2. Combine the salad: In a large bowl, add the chickpeas, cucumber, bell pepper, red onion, feta cheese, and parsley.
3. Make the dressing: In a small bowl, whisk together the olive oil, lemon juice, oregano, garlic powder, salt, and pepper.
4. Dress the salad: Pour the dressing over the salad and toss gently to coat all ingredients.
5. Chill and serve: Refrigerate for at least 30 minutes for the flavors to meld. Serve chilled or at room temperature.

Nutritional Information: Calories: 300, Carbohydrates: 30g, Fiber: 8g, Net Carbs: 22g, Protein: 15g, Fat: 10g, Sodium: 250mg

Tips:
- For extra protein and texture, roast half of the chickpeas before adding them to the salad.
- Use low-fat or fat-free feta cheese to reduce the sodium and fat content.
- Add other chopped vegetables like celery, carrots, or zucchini for additional variety.
- Serve the salad on a bed of leafy greens for added fiber and nutrients.
- Adjust the amount of dressing to your liking.
- Store leftover salad in an airtight container in the refrigerator for up to 3 days.

Vegetable and Tofu Stir-Fry

Prep Time: 15 minutes | **Cooking Time**: 15 minutes | **Total Time**: 30 minutes | **Serving Size**: 2

Ingredients:
For the tofu:
- 14 oz. extra firm tofu, drained and cubed
- 1 tbsp. low-sodium soy sauce
- 1 tsp. cornstarch
- 1/2 tsp. ground ginger
- 1 tbsp. vegetable oil

For the stir-fry:
- 1 cup broccoli florets
- 1 cup bell pepper (any color), sliced
- 1 cup snow peas
- 1/2 cup sliced carrots
- 1/4 cup chopped onion
- 2 cloves garlic, minced
- 1 tbsp. low-sodium soy sauce
- 1 tbsp. rice vinegar
- 1 tsp. sesame oil
- 1/2 tsp. sriracha (optional)
- 1/4 cup cooked brown rice or quinoa (optional)
- Sesame seeds and chopped green onions, for garnish

Directions:
1. Marinate the tofu: In a bowl, whisk together soy sauce, cornstarch, and ginger. Add tofu cubes and toss to coat. Let marinate for at least 15 minutes.
2. Prepare the vegetables: Wash and chop all vegetables.
3. Cook the tofu: Heat oil in a large skillet or wok over medium-high heat. Drain the tofu cubes and add them to the pan. Cook for 5-7 minutes per side, until golden brown and crispy. Remove from the pan and set aside.
4. Stir-fry the vegetables: Add a little more oil to the pan if needed. Add onion and garlic, cook for 30 seconds. Add bell peppers, broccoli, and carrots, cook for 2-3 minutes until slightly softened. Add snow peas and cook for another minute.
5. Combine and finish: Stir in the soy sauce, rice vinegar, sesame oil, and sriracha (if using). Add the cooked tofu back to the pan and toss to coat. Heat for another minute.
6. Serve: Divide the stir-fry between two plates. Top with cooked brown rice or quinoa (optional) and garnish with sesame seeds and green onions.

Nutritional Information: Calories: 400, Carbohydrates: 30g, Fiber: 8g, Protein: 20g, Fat: 15g, Sodium: 300mg

Tips:
Use non-stick cooking spray instead of oil for a lower-fat option.
Add other vegetables of your choice, such as zucchini, mushrooms, or snap peas.
Top with chopped peanuts or cashews for added protein and crunch.
Adjust the amount of sriracha to your spice preference.
Serve with a side salad for a more complete meal.

Caprese Chicken Salad

Prep Time: 10 minutes | **Cooking Time**: 15 minutes | **Total Time**: 25 minutes | **Servings**: 1

Ingredients:
- 4 oz. boneless, skinless chicken breast, grilled or baked
- 1 medium tomato, sliced
- 1/2 cup baby spinach or mixed greens
- 1/4 cup mozzarella cheese, cubed
- 1/4 cup cherry tomatoes, halved (optional)
- 1 tbsp. olive oil
- 1 tbsp. balsamic vinegar
- 1/4 tsp. dried oregano
- Salt and pepper to taste
- Fresh basil leaves, for garnish

Directions:
1. Prepare the chicken: If grilling, preheat grill to medium-high heat. Grill chicken for 5-7 minutes per side, or until cooked through. If baking, preheat oven to 400°F (200°C). Bake chicken for 15-20 minutes, or until cooked through. Let cool slightly and slice or shred.
2. Assemble the salad: In a bowl, combine baby spinach or mixed greens with sliced tomato, mozzarella cheese, and cherry tomatoes (if using).
3. Make the dressing: Whisk together olive oil, balsamic vinegar, oregano, salt, and pepper.
4. Top the salad: Drizzle the dressing over the salad and add the sliced or shredded chicken.
5. Garnish: Top with fresh basil leaves and enjoy

Nutritional Information: Calories: 350, Carbohydrates: 15g, Fiber: 2g, Net Carbs: 13g Protein: 30g, Fat: 15g

Tips:
- For a lower-carb option, use cherry tomatoes instead of regular tomatoes.
- You can add other vegetables to the salad, such as cucumbers, bell peppers, or olives.
- If you don't have fresh basil, you can use dried basil or another herb, such as oregano or thyme.
- Feel free to adjust the amount of dressing to your preference.
- This recipe is easily doubled or tripled to serve more people.
- If you have leftover chicken, you can store it in the refrigerator for up to 3 days and reheat it before adding it to the salad.

Whole Wheat Pasta with Pesto and Vegetables

Prep Time: 10 minutes | **Cooking Time**: 12 minutes | **Total Time**: 22 minutes | **Serving Size**: 1 person

Ingredients:
- 2 ounces whole wheat pasta (such as penne, fusilli, or rotini)
- 1 cup mixed vegetables (such as broccoli, cherry tomatoes, zucchini, and bell peppers)
- ¼ cup prepared pesto (homemade or store-bought, choose reduced-sodium if available)
- 1 tablespoon olive oil
- ½ cup low-sodium chicken or vegetable broth
- ¼ cup crumbled feta cheese (optional)
- Fresh basil leaves, for garnish (optional)
- Salt and pepper to taste

Directions:
1. Cook the pasta: Bring a pot of salted water to a boil. Add the pasta and cook according to package instructions until al dente. Drain and set aside.
2. Prepare the vegetables: While the pasta is cooking, wash and chop the vegetables into bite-sized pieces. Heat the olive oil in a large skillet over medium heat. Add the vegetables and cook for 5-7 minutes, or until tender-crisp.
3. Combine everything: Add the cooked pasta, pesto, and broth to the skillet with the vegetables. Toss to coat everything evenly. Heat through for 1-2 minutes, stirring occasionally.
4. Serve and enjoy: Divide the pasta mixture between two plates. Top with crumbled feta cheese and fresh basil leaves, if desired. Season with additional salt and pepper to taste.

Nutritional Information: Calories: 450, Carbohydrates: 50g, Fiber: 8g, Protein: 15g, Fat: 15g, Sodium: 350mg

Tips:
- For added protein, include grilled chicken breast, shrimp, or tofu.
- Substitute different vegetables based on your preference and seasonality.
- Use a homemade pesto if you have the time and fresh herbs available.
- To make this recipe vegan, omit the feta cheese and use a vegan pesto.
- Leftovers can be stored in an airtight container in the refrigerator for up to 3 days.

Shrimp and Avocado Lettuce Wraps

Prep Time: 10 minutes | **Cooking Time**: 8 minutes | **Total Time**: 18 minutes | **Servings**: 2

Ingredients:
- 1 pound large shrimp, peeled and deveined
- 1 tablespoon olive oil
- 1/2 teaspoon garlic powder
- 1/4 teaspoon paprika
- 1/4 teaspoon chili powder (optional)
- Salt and pepper to taste
- 4 large romaine lettuce leaves, washed and dried
- 1 avocado, diced
- 1/2 red onion, thinly sliced
- 1/4 cup crumbled feta cheese (optional)
- 1/4 cup chopped fresh cilantro
- Lime wedges, for serving

Directions:
1. Marinate the shrimp: In a bowl, combine olive oil, garlic powder, paprika, chili powder (if using), salt, and pepper. Add the shrimp and toss to coat. Marinate for at least 10 minutes, or up to 30 minutes.
2. Cook the shrimp: Heat a large skillet over medium-high heat. Add the shrimp and cook for 3-4 minutes per side, or until pink and cooked through. Be careful not to overcook them, as they will become tough.
3. Assemble the wraps: Place a romaine lettuce leaf on a plate. Top with some cooked shrimp, avocado, red onion, and feta cheese (if using). Sprinkle with cilantro and drizzle with lime juice.
4. Wrap the lettuce leaf around the filling and take a bite.

Nutritional Information: Calories: 350, Carbohydrates: 15g, Fiber: 3g, Net Carbs: 12g, Protein: 30g, Fat: 15g, Sodium: 300mg

Tips:
- For a spicier wrap, add a pinch of red pepper flakes to the marinade.
- Use low-sodium soy sauce to reduce the sodium content.
- If you don't have romaine lettuce, you can use other large lettuce leaves like butter lettuce or Bibb lettuce.
- You can add other vegetables to the wraps, such as cucumber, shredded carrots, or bell peppers.
- This recipe is easily doubled or tripled to feed more people.

Stuffed Bell Peppers

Prep Time: 15 minutes | **Cooking Time**: 45 minutes | **Total Time**: 60 minutes | **Serving Size**: 2

Ingredients:
- 2 large bell peppers (red, green, or a mix)
- 1 tablespoon olive oil
- 1 medium onion, diced
- 2 cloves garlic, minced
- 1/2 cup ground turkey or lean chicken breast
- 1/2 cup chopped mushrooms
- 1/4 cup diced zucchini
- 1/4 cup chopped sun-dried tomatoes
- 1/2 cup cooked quinoa or brown rice
- 1/4 cup crumbled feta cheese
- 1/4 cup chopped fresh parsley
- 1/2 teaspoon dried oregano
- 1/4 teaspoon dried thyme
- Salt and black pepper to taste

Directions:
1. Prep the Peppers: Preheat oven to 375°F (190°C). Wash and dry the bell peppers. Cut them in half lengthwise and remove the seeds and membranes. Place the peppers cut-side up in a baking dish.
2. Cook the Filling: Heat olive oil in a pan over medium heat. Add onion and cook until softened, about 5 minutes. Add garlic and cook for another minute. Increase heat to medium-high and add ground turkey or chicken. Brown the meat, breaking it up with a spoon.
3. Add Veggies and Spices: Stir in mushrooms, zucchini, and sun-dried tomatoes. Cook for 5 minutes, or until vegetables are softened. Add quinoa or brown rice, oregano, thyme, salt, and pepper. Mix well.
4. Stuff and Bake: Spoon the filling evenly into the bell pepper halves. Top with feta cheese and parsley. Bake for 45 minutes, or until the peppers are tender and the filling is cooked through.
5. Let the peppers cool slightly before serving.

Nutritional Information: Calories: 350, Carbohydrates: 30g, Fiber: 8g, Net Carbs: 22g, Protein: 20g, Fat: 15g

Tips:
- For a vegetarian option, replace the ground meat with lentils or black beans.
- You can add a small amount of low-sodium tomato sauce to the filling for extra moisture.
- If you don't have fresh herbs, use 1/2 teaspoon each of dried oregano and thyme.
- Feel free to adjust the spices and seasonings to your liking.
- For added protein, serve with a Greek yogurt sauce or a side of non-starchy vegetables.

DINNER IDEAS

Grilled Chicken Breast with Roasted Vegetables

Prep Time: 15 minutes | **Cooking Time**: 30 minutes | **Total Time**: 45 minutes | **Serving Size**: 2

Ingredients:
For the Chicken:
- 2 boneless, skinless chicken breasts
- 1 tablespoon olive oil
- 1/2 teaspoon dried oregano
- 1/2 teaspoon garlic powder
- 1/4 teaspoon salt
- 1/4 teaspoon black pepper

For the Vegetables:
- 1 bell pepper, any color, sliced
- 1 zucchini, sliced
- 1 onion, sliced
- 1 cup broccoli florets
- 1/2 cup cherry tomatoes
- 1 tablespoon olive oil
- 1/4 teaspoon dried thyme
- 1/4 teaspoon salt
- 1/4 teaspoon black pepper

Directions:
1. Preheat the oven to 400°F (200°C). Line a baking sheet with parchment paper.
2. Prepare the chicken: Combine olive oil, oregano, garlic powder, salt, and pepper in a small bowl. Rub the mixture on both sides of the chicken breasts.
3. Prepare the vegetables: Toss the bell pepper, zucchini, onion, broccoli florets, and cherry tomatoes with olive oil, thyme, salt, and pepper.
4. Arrange the vegetables on the prepared baking sheet and place the chicken on top.
5. Bake for 25-30 minutes, or until the chicken is cooked through and the vegetables are tender. An instant-read thermometer inserted into the thickest part of the chicken should reach 165°F (74°C).
6. Serve immediately and enjoy.

Nutritional Information: Calories: 400, Carbohydrates: 20g, Fiber: 5g, Protein: 35g, Fat: 10g

Tips:
- You can use any type of vegetables you like in this recipe. Just be sure to adjust the cooking time if necessary.
- For added flavor, marinate the chicken in your favorite marinade for at least 30 minutes before grilling.
- Serve the chicken and vegetables with a side of brown rice or quinoa for a more complete meal.
- Be sure to check the nutritional labels of any additional ingredients you use, such as marinades or sauces, to ensure they are diabetic-friendly.

Salmon and Asparagus Foil Packets

Prep Time: 10 minutes | **Cooking Time**: 20 minutes | **Total Time**: 30 minutes | **Servings**: 4

Ingredients:
- 4 (6-ounce) skinless salmon fillets
- 1 pound asparagus, trimmed and ends snapped off
- 1/4 cup fresh lemon juice
- 2 tablespoons olive oil
- 2 cloves garlic, minced
- 1/2 teaspoon dried thyme
- 1/4 teaspoon dried oregano
- 1/4 teaspoon black pepper
- 1/8 teaspoon salt (adjust to taste)
- 1/4 cup chopped fresh parsley (optional, for garnish)

Directions:
1. Preheat oven to 400°F (200°C).
2. Cut four 12-inch squares of aluminum foil. Place each salmon fillet in the center of a foil square.
3. Arrange asparagus spears evenly next to each salmon fillet.
4. In a small bowl, whisk together lemon juice, olive oil, garlic, thyme, oregano, pepper, and salt.
5. Drizzle the herb mixture evenly over the salmon and asparagus.
6. Fold the foil squares up and over the ingredients, crimping the edges to create sealed packets. Leave a small vent at the top of each packet to allow steam to escape.
7. Place the foil packets on a baking sheet and bake for 20 minutes, or until the salmon is cooked through and flakes easily with a fork.
8. Carefully open the foil packets and garnish with fresh parsley, if desired.

Nutritional Information: Calories: 350, Protein: 30g, Fat: 15g, Carbohydrates: 10g, Sodium: 300mg

Tips:
- For a crispy topping, broil the packets for an additional 2-3 minutes after baking.
- Add other vegetables to the packets, such as cherry tomatoes, bell peppers, or zucchini.
- Substitute cod or another lean white fish for the salmon.
- Use low-sodium soy sauce instead of salt for a different flavor profile.
- Adjust the seasonings to your taste preferences.

Vegetarian Quinoa Stir-Fry

Prep Time: 15 minutes | **Cooking Time**: 20 minutes | **Total Time**: 35 minutes | **Servings**: 4

Ingredients:
- 1 cup quinoa, rinsed
- 2 cups vegetable broth
- 1 tablespoon olive oil
- 1 teaspoon sesame oil
- 1 onion, diced
- 2 cloves garlic, minced
- 1 bell pepper, sliced
- 1 cup broccoli florets
- 1/2 cup snow peas
- 1/2 cup carrots, shredded
- 1/4 cup shelled peas (fresh or frozen)
- 2 tablespoons low-sodium soy sauce (or tamari or coconut aminos)
- 1 tablespoon rice vinegar
- 1 tablespoon sriracha (optional, for heat)
- 1/2 teaspoon ground ginger
- Salt and pepper to taste
- Chopped fresh cilantro, for garnish (optional)

Directions:
1. Cook the quinoa: In a medium saucepan, combine quinoa and vegetable broth. Bring to a boil, then reduce heat, cover, and simmer for 15 minutes, or until all the liquid is absorbed. Fluff with a fork and set aside.
2. Prepare the vegetables: While the quinoa cooks, heat olive oil and sesame oil in a large skillet or wok over medium-high heat. Add the onion and cook until softened, about 5 minutes. Add the garlic and cook for another minute, until fragrant.
3. Add the bell pepper and broccoli: Stir in the bell pepper and broccoli florets. Cook for 3-4 minutes, until the broccoli is slightly tender.
4. Incorporate remaining vegetables: Add the snow peas, carrots, and peas. Cook for another 2-3 minutes, until the vegetables are crisp-tender.
5. Make the sauce: In a small bowl, whisk together soy sauce, rice vinegar, sriracha (if using), and ginger.
6. Combine and finish: Stir the cooked quinoa into the pan with the vegetables. Pour in the sauce and toss to coat everything evenly. Cook for another minute or two, until heated through.
7. Serve: Plate the stir-fry and garnish with chopped fresh cilantro, if desired.

Nutritional Information: Calories: 350, Carbohydrates: 40g, Fiber: 8g, Protein: 15g, Fat: 10g, Sodium: 300mg

Tips:
- For a heartier stir-fry, add cooked tofu or tempeh.
- Serve over brown rice or another whole grain for additional fiber and nutrients.
- Adjust the amount of sriracha to your desired level of spiciness.
- Feel free to substitute different vegetables based on your preference and what's in season.
- To make this stir-fry ahead of time, cook the quinoa and vegetables separately and store them in airtight containers in the refrigerator. Assemble and heat through when ready to serve.

Turkey and Vegetable Skewers

Prep Time: 15 minutes | **Cooking Time**: 15-20 minutes | **Total Time**: 30-35 minutes | **Servings**: 4

Ingredients:

1 pound boneless, skinless turkey breast, cut into 1-inch cubes
1 bell pepper, cut into 1-inch squares
1 red onion, cut into 1-inch wedges
1 zucchini, cut into 1-inch rounds
1 cup cherry tomatoes
1/4 cup olive oil
2 tablespoons lemon juice
1 tablespoon balsamic vinegar
1 teaspoon dried oregano
1/2 teaspoon garlic powder
1/4 teaspoon black pepper
Salt to taste (optional)
Wooden skewers (soaked in water for 30 minutes to prevent burning)

Directions:
1. Marinate the turkey: In a large bowl, whisk together olive oil, lemon juice, balsamic vinegar, oregano, garlic powder, and black pepper. Add the turkey cubes and toss to coat evenly. Cover and refrigerate for at least 30 minutes, or up to 4 hours.
2. Assemble the skewers: Thread turkey cubes, bell pepper squares, red onion wedges, zucchini rounds, and cherry tomatoes onto soaked wooden skewers, alternating ingredients for visual appeal.
3. Cook the skewers: Preheat your grill or grill pan to medium-high heat. Grill the skewers for 10-12 minutes per side, or until the turkey is cooked through and the vegetables are tender-crisp.
4. Serve: Remove the skewers from the heat and let them cool slightly before serving. Enjoy immediately with a side of low-carb vegetables or a whole-wheat pita bread.

Nutritional Information: Calories: 300, Carbohydrates: 20g, Fiber: 5g, Protein: 30g, Fat: 10g, Saturated Fat: 2g, Sodium: 400mg

Tips:
- For a smoky flavor, add a teaspoon of smoked paprika to the marinade.
- If you don't have a grill, you can bake the skewers in a preheated oven at 400°F for 20-25 minutes, flipping halfway through.
- Make sure to choose low-sodium marinades or dressings to keep the sodium content in check.
- Use a variety of colorful vegetables to add visual interest and different nutrients.
- You can substitute lean chicken or ground turkey for the turkey breast.
- For a more filling meal, serve the skewers with a side of quinoa or brown rice.

Cauliflower Fried Rice with Shrimp

Prep Time: 10 minutes | **Cooking Time**: 15 minutes | **Total Time**: 25 minutes | **Servings**: 2

Ingredients:
- 1 head cauliflower, riced (about 4 cups)
- 1/2 tablespoon olive oil
- 1/4 teaspoon sesame oil
- 1/2 red bell pepper, diced
- 1/2 cup broccoli florets, chopped
- 1/4 cup green onion, chopped
- 3 cloves garlic, minced
- 1 tablespoon grated ginger
- 1/2 pound shrimp, peeled and deveined
- 2 large eggs, beaten
- 2 tablespoons reduced-sodium soy sauce
- 1 tablespoon lime juice
- 1/4 teaspoon black pepper
- Chopped fresh cilantro, for garnish (optional)

Directions:
1. Prep the cauliflower rice: If you don't have pre-riced cauliflower, pulse the florets in a food processor until rice-like consistency.
2. Heat the oils: In a large skillet or wok, heat olive oil and sesame oil over medium-high heat.
3. Sauté the vegetables: Add the bell pepper, broccoli, and green onion. Cook for 3-4 minutes, stirring occasionally, until softened slightly.
4. Add aromatics: Stir in the garlic and ginger. Cook for another minute until fragrant.
5. Cook the shrimp: Add the shrimp and cook for 2-3 minutes per side, or until pink and cooked through. Remove from the pan and set aside.
6. Scramble the eggs: Push the vegetables to one side of the pan and pour in the beaten eggs. Scramble until just set.
7. Incorporate cauliflower rice: Add the cauliflower rice and stir-fry for 2-3 minutes, until heated through.
8. Combine and season: Return the shrimp to the pan and mix with the cauliflower rice, vegetables, and eggs. Pour in the soy sauce, lime juice, and black pepper. Toss to coat everything evenly.
9. Garnish and serve: Remove from heat and garnish with chopped cilantro, if desired. Serve immediately.

Nutritional Information: Calories: 320, Carbohydrates: 15g, Net carbs: 8g, Protein: 30g, Fat: 12g, Sodium: 400mg

Tips:
- Use low-sodium soy sauce or tamari to further reduce sodium content.
- Add other vegetables like carrots, peas, or snow peas for variety.
- Adjust the amount of soy sauce to your taste preference.
- Serve with a side of steamed or roasted vegetables for a complete meal.
- If you have leftover cooked shrimp, you can use that instead of cooking fresh shrimp.

Lemon Herb Baked Cod with Sweet Potato Mash

Prep Time: 15 minutes | **Cooking Time**: 25 minutes | **Total Time**: 40 minutes **Servings**: 4

Ingredients:

For the Cod:
- 4 cod fillets (about 6 ounces each)
- 1 tablespoon olive oil
- 1/2 teaspoon dried thyme
- 1/4 teaspoon dried oregano
- 1/4 teaspoon garlic powder
- 1/4 teaspoon black pepper
- 1/4 cup fresh lemon juice
- 2 tablespoons chopped fresh parsley (optional)

For the Sweet Potato Mash:
- 2 large sweet potatoes, peeled and diced
- 1/2 cup unsweetened almond milk
- 1 tablespoon olive oil
- 1/4 teaspoon cinnamon
- 1/4 teaspoon ground ginger
- Salt and pepper to taste

Directions:
1. Preheat oven to 400°F (200°C).
2. Prepare the Cod: In a small bowl, whisk together olive oil, thyme, oregano, garlic powder, and black pepper. Rub the mixture onto the cod fillets.
3. Place the cod fillets in a baking dish and drizzle with lemon juice.
4. Bake for 15-20 minutes, or until the cod is cooked through and flakes easily with a fork.
5. Prepare the Sweet Potato Mash: While the cod is baking, cook the sweet potatoes in boiling water until tender, about 10-15 minutes.
6. Drain the sweet potatoes and return them to the pot. Mash with almond milk, olive oil, cinnamon, and ginger until smooth. Season with salt and pepper to taste.
7. Serve the cod fillets with the sweet potato mash and garnish with fresh parsley, if desired.

Nutritional Information: Calories: 450, Carbohydrates: 35g, Fiber: 5g, Protein: 40g, Fat: 15g, Sodium: 400mg

Tips:
- To make this dish even more diabetic-friendly, use low-sodium soy sauce instead of salt.
- You can also add other vegetables to the sweet potato mash, such as carrots, broccoli, or spinach.
- This recipe is easily doubled or tripled to feed a crowd.
- For a richer flavor, you can use full-fat coconut milk instead of almond milk in the sweet potato mash. However, this will increase the calorie and fat content.

Chickpea and Spinach Curry

Prep Time: 10 minutes | **Cooking Time**: 30 minutes | **Total Time**: 40 minutes | **Servings**: 4

Ingredients:

- 1 tablespoon olive oil
- 1 medium onion, chopped
- 2 cloves garlic, minced
- 1 tablespoon grated ginger
- 1 teaspoon ground cumin
- 1 teaspoon ground coriander
- 1/2 teaspoon turmeric
- 1/4 teaspoon chili powder (optional)
- 1 (14.5 oz.) can diced tomatoes, undrained
- 1 (13.5 oz.) can vegetable broth
- 1 (15 oz.) can chickpeas, drained and rinsed
- 5 cups baby spinach
- 1/4 cup chopped fresh cilantro (optional)
- 1/4 teaspoon salt (or to taste)
- Cooked brown rice, quinoa, or whole-wheat roti for serving

Directions:

1. Heat oil in a large pot or Dutch oven over medium heat. Add onion and cook until softened, about 5 minutes. Stir in garlic and ginger, cook for an additional minute.
2. Add cumin, coriander, turmeric, and chili powder (if using). Cook for 30 seconds, stirring constantly, to release the aromas of the spices.
3. Pour in diced tomatoes and vegetable broth. Bring to a boil, then reduce heat to simmer. Cook for 10 minutes.
4. Stir in chickpeas and spinach. Cook for 5 minutes, or until spinach is wilted.
5. Remove from heat and stir in cilantro (if using) and salt to taste.

Nutritional Information: Calories: 320, Carbohydrates: 40g, Fiber: 8g, Protein: 15g, Fat: 10g, Sodium: 350mg

Tips:

- For a richer flavor, use coconut milk instead of vegetable broth.
- Add other vegetables like chopped bell peppers, carrots, or zucchini.
- Adjust the amount of chili powder according to your spice preference.
- Serve with a side of low-fat yogurt or raita for added protein and calcium.
- Leftovers can be stored in an airtight container in the refrigerator for up to 3 days.

Stuffed Bell Peppers with Ground Turkey

Prep Time: 15 minutes | **Cooking Time**: 45 minutes | **Total Time**: 60 minutes | **Servings**: 4

Nutritional Information: Calories: 350, Carbohydrates: 30g, Fiber: 5g, Protein: 30g, Fat: 15g, Sodium: 400mg

Ingredients:
- 4 large bell peppers, any color combination
- 1 tablespoon olive oil
- 1 pound lean ground turkey
- 1/2 onion, chopped
- 2 cloves garlic, minced
- 1 teaspoon dried oregano
- 1/2 teaspoon ground cumin
- 1/4 teaspoon chili powder
- Salt and pepper to taste
- 1 (14.5 oz.) can diced tomatoes, undrained
- 1/2 cup cooked quinoa or brown rice
- 1/4 cup chopped fresh parsley
- 1/2 cup shredded low-fat cheddar cheese

Directions:
1. Preheat oven to 375°F (190°C).
2. Wash and halve the bell peppers lengthwise, removing the seeds and membranes. Place them in a baking dish.
3. Heat olive oil in a large skillet over medium heat. Add the ground turkey and cook, breaking it up with a spoon, until browned.
4. Stir in the onion, garlic, oregano, cumin, chili powder, salt, and pepper. Cook for 5 minutes, or until the onion is softened.
5. Stir in the diced tomatoes and quinoa or brown rice. Bring to a simmer and cook for 5 minutes more.
6. Remove from heat and stir in the parsley.
7. Divide the filling evenly among the bell pepper halves. Sprinkle with cheddar cheese.
8. Bake for 30-35 minutes, or until the peppers are tender and the cheese is melted.

Nutritional Information: Calories: 320, Carbohydrates: 40g, Fiber: 8g, Protein: 15g, Fat: 10g, Sodium: 350mg

Tips:
- To make this recipe even more diabetic-friendly, use a low-sodium tomato sauce and cheese.
- You can also substitute ground chicken or ground beef for the ground turkey.
- If you don't have quinoa or brown rice, you can use cauliflower rice instead.
- For a vegetarian option, use lentils or black beans instead of ground meat.
- Serve with a side salad or roasted vegetables for a complete meal.

Eggplant and Zucchini Lasagna

Prep Time: 40 minutes | **Cooking Time**: 50 minutes | **Total Time**: 1 hour 30 minutes | **Servings**: 4-6

Ingredients:
Vegetables:
- 1 large eggplant, sliced 1/4-inch thick
- 2 medium zucchini, sliced 1/4-inch thick
- 1 tablespoon olive oil
- 1/2 teaspoon salt
- 1/4 teaspoon black pepper

Sauce:
- 1 tablespoon olive oil
- 1 onion, chopped
- 2 cloves garlic, minced
- 1 (28-ounce) can crushed tomatoes
- 1/2 teaspoon dried oregano
- 1/4 teaspoon dried basil
- Salt and pepper to taste

Cheese Filling:
- 15 ounces ricotta cheese, part-skim
- 1/4 cup grated Parmesan cheese
- 1/4 cup chopped fresh basil
- 1/4 teaspoon salt
- 1/4 teaspoon black pepper

Topping:
- 1/4 cup grated mozzarella cheese

Directions:
1. Preheat oven to 375°F (190°C). Line a 9x13 inch baking dish with parchment paper.
2. Prepare the vegetables: Arrange eggplant slices on a baking sheet and sprinkle with 1/2 teaspoon salt. Let sit for 15 minutes, then pat dry with paper towels. Repeat with zucchini slices, using remaining salt. Brush both sides of vegetables with olive oil and season with pepper.
3. Roast the vegetables: Bake eggplant for 15 minutes, then flip and bake for an additional 10 minutes. Bake zucchini for 10 minutes per side. Let cool slightly.
4. Make the sauce: Heat olive oil in a large saucepan over medium heat. Add onion and cook until softened, about 5 minutes. Add garlic and cook for an additional minute. Stir in crushed tomatoes, oregano, basil, salt, and pepper. Bring to a simmer and cook for 20 minutes, stirring occasionally.
5. Prepare the cheese filling: In a bowl, combine ricotta cheese, Parmesan cheese, basil, salt, and pepper.
6. Assemble the lasagna: Spread a thin layer of sauce on the bottom of the baking dish. Top with a layer of roasted eggplant slices, then a layer of ricotta cheese filling. Repeat with another layer of sauce, zucchini slices, and ricotta cheese filling. Finish with a final layer of sauce and sprinkle with mozzarella cheese.
7. Bake the lasagna: Cover the dish with foil and bake for 20 minutes. Uncover and bake for an additional 10 minutes, or until heated through and cheese is golden brown.
8. Let cool and serve: Allow the lasagna to cool for 10 minutes before slicing and serving.

Nutritional Information: Calories: 350, Carbohydrates: 30g, Fiber: 5g, Protein: 20g Fat: 15g, Sodium: 500mg

Tips:
- For a richer flavor, add 1/4 cup ground lean sausage to the sauce while cooking.
- To make this recipe vegan, use vegan ricotta cheese and mozzarella cheese alternatives.
- Leftovers can be stored in the refrigerator for up to 3 days.

Beef and Vegetable Stir-Fry with Brown Rice

Prep Time: 15 minutes | **Cooking Time**: 20 minutes | **Total Time**: 35 minutes **Servings**: 4

Ingredients:
For the Brown Rice:
- 1 cup brown rice, rinsed
- 2 cups water

For the Stir-Fry:
- 1 pound flank steak, thinly sliced
- 1 tablespoon cornstarch
- 1 tablespoon low-sodium soy sauce
- 1 tablespoon rice vinegar
- 1 teaspoon sesame oil
- 1/2 teaspoon minced ginger
- 1 clove garlic, minced
- 1 red bell pepper, sliced
- 1 green bell pepper, sliced
- 1 cup broccoli florets
- 1/2 cup baby carrots, sliced
- 1/4 cup sugar snap peas
- 1/4 cup chopped green onions
- 1 tablespoon vegetable oil

Directions:
1. Cook the Brown Rice: Rinse the brown rice and add it to a pot with 2 cups of water. Bring to a boil, then reduce heat, cover, and simmer for 45 minutes, or until cooked through.
2. Marinate the Beef: In a bowl, combine cornstarch, soy sauce, rice vinegar, sesame oil, ginger, and garlic. Add the sliced beef and toss to coat. Marinate for at least 15 minutes, while preparing the vegetables.
3. Prepare the Vegetables: Wash and slice the bell peppers, broccoli, carrots, and sugar snap peas. Chop the green onions.
4. Cook the Stir-Fry: Heat the vegetable oil in a large skillet or wok over high heat. Add the beef and cook, stirring occasionally, until browned (about 3-4 minutes). Remove the beef from the pan and set aside.
5. Sauté the Vegetables: Add the bell peppers, broccoli, and carrots to the pan and cook for 3-4 minutes, until slightly softened. Add the sugar snap peas and cook for an additional 1-2 minutes.
6. Return the Beef and Sauce: Return the cooked beef to the pan with the vegetables. Pour in any remaining marinade from the bowl.
7. Thicken the Sauce: In a small bowl, whisk together 1 tablespoon of cornstarch with 2 tablespoons of water to make a slurry. Add the slurry to the pan and stir until the sauce thickens.
8. Serve: Serve the stir-fry over cooked brown rice and garnish with chopped green onions.

Nutritional Information: Calories: 400, Carbohydrates: 40g, Fiber: 5g, Protein: 30g, Fat: 15g, Sodium: 500mg

Tips:
- Use lean cuts of beef, such as flank steak or sirloin.
- Choose low-sodium soy sauce to reduce sodium content.
- Add other non-starchy vegetables, such as zucchini, snow peas, or mushrooms.
- Serve with a side of low-fat yogurt or cottage cheese for additional protein.
- Adjust the amount of sauce and cornstarch to your desired consistency.
- Taste and adjust seasonings as needed before serving.

QUICK AND EASY SNACKS

Greek Yogurt with Berries

Prep Time: 5 minutes | **Cooking Time**: 0 minutes | **Total Time**: 5 minutes | **Serving Size**: 1

Ingredients:

- 1 cup plain Greek yogurt (unsweetened or low-fat)
- 1/2 cup fresh berries (any combination you like: blueberries, raspberries, strawberries, etc.)
- 1/4 cup chopped nuts or seeds (almonds, walnuts, chia seeds, flaxseeds, etc.)
- Optional: 1/4 teaspoon ground cinnamon, 1 tablespoon sugar-free sweetener (if needed)

Directions:

1. In a bowl, combine the Greek yogurt.
2. Add the berries and gently fold them in to avoid mashing them.
3. Sprinkle the chopped nuts or seeds on top.
4. For additional sweetness and flavor, add cinnamon or sugar-free sweetener (if desired).
5. Enjoy immediately

Nutritional Information: Calories: 140, Carbohydrates: 15g, Protein: 15g, Fat: 5g, Fiber: 3g, Sugar: 8g

Tips:

- Use unsweetened or low-fat Greek yogurt to minimize added sugar.
- Choose berries with a low glycemic index to prevent blood sugar spikes. Some good options include blueberries, raspberries, and strawberries.
- For extra protein and healthy fats, add a scoop of peanut butter or almond butter.
- Prepare individual portions in small containers for easy grab-and-go snacks.
- Freeze the berries beforehand for a refreshing frozen yogurt-like treat.
- Experiment with different toppings like shredded coconut, dark chocolate chips, or a drizzle of honey (use sparingly).

Vegetable Sticks with Hummus

Prep Time: 10 minutes | **Cooking Time**: 0 minutes | **Total Time**: 10 minutes | **Serving Size**: 1-2

Ingredients:

- 1 cup assorted vegetables, cut into sticks (e.g., cucumber, carrot, bell pepper, celery)
- 1/2 cup hummus (plain or flavored)
- Optional: Sprinkle of herbs and spices (e.g., paprika, cumin, chili flakes)

Directions:

1. Wash and dry all vegetables. Cut them into sticks of similar size, making them easy to dip.
2. Place the hummus in a serving bowl. If using store-bought hummus, you may want to stir it to loosen it up.
3. Arrange the vegetable sticks around the hummus bowl.
4. Sprinkle with herbs and spices, if desired.

Nutritional Information: Calories: 200-300, Carbohydrates: 15-20g, Fiber: 5-7g, Protein: 5-7g, Fat: 5-7g

Tips:

- Choose vegetables with low glycemic index (GI) scores, such as cucumber, carrot, and bell pepper.
- For a more filling snack, add whole-wheat pita bread or crackers.
- Make sure to portion control, especially if you are counting carbohydrates.
- Experiment with different flavors of hummus to find your favorites.
- If you have time, you can roast the vegetables for a slightly different flavor and texture.
- You can also add a dollop of plain Greek yogurt to the hummus for extra protein and creaminess.
- Store leftover vegetable sticks in an airtight container in the refrigerator for up to 3 days. Hummus can be stored in the refrigerator for up to 5 days.

Hard-Boiled Eggs

Prep Time: 5 minutes | **Cooking Time**: 12-15 minutes | **Total Time**: 17-20 minutes | **Serving Size**: 1-2

Ingredients:
- Eggs (fresh and preferably at room temperature)
- Water
- Optional: Vinegar (a splash helps loosen the shells)

Directions:

1. Place the eggs in a single layer in a saucepan. Cover with cold water, ensuring at least 1 inch of water above the eggs. You can add a splash of vinegar if desired.
2. Bring the water to a boil over high heat. Once boiling, immediately remove the pan from the heat and cover.
3. Set a timer for 12-15 minutes depending on your desired level of doneness:
4. 12 minutes: Slightly soft yolk with a runny center.
5. 13-14 minutes: Moderately firm yolk.
6. 15 minutes: Completely firm yolk.
7. After the timer goes off, immediately drain the hot water and run cold water over the eggs for a few minutes. This helps stop the cooking process and makes peeling easier.
8. Peel the eggs carefully under running water. You can crack the shells gently beforehand for easier peeling.
9. Enjoy your hard-boiled eggs plain or with your favorite toppings

Nutritional Information: Calories: 78 Protein: 6.3g, Fat: 5g, Carbohydrates: 0.6 g
Cholesterol: 212 mg, Sodium: 63 mg

Tips:

- For easier peeling, use older eggs (a few days old).
- Crack the shells slightly before cooking to allow some air to escape, making peeling easier.
- Shock the eggs in an ice bath after cooking for a super smooth and easy peel.
- Store hard-boiled eggs in an airtight container in the refrigerator for up to 5 days.

Nuts and Seeds Mix

Prep Time: 5 minutes | **Cooking Time**: 0 minutes | **Total Time**: 5 minutes | **Serving Size**: 1/4 cup

Ingredients:
- 1/2 cup raw almonds
- 1/4 cup raw walnuts
- 1/4 cup raw pecans
- 1/4 cup raw pistachios
- 1/4 cup pumpkin seeds
- 1/4 cup sunflower seeds
- 1/4 cup flaxseeds
- 1/4 cup dried cranberries (optional, use unsweetened or lightly sweetened)
- 1/4 teaspoon ground cinnamon (optional)
- Pinch of sea salt (optional)

Directions:
1. Measure and toast (optional): Measure out all of your ingredients. If desired, toast the nuts and seeds in a dry skillet over medium heat for a few minutes, stirring constantly, until slightly browned and fragrant. Be careful not to burn them.
2. Combine: In a large bowl, combine all of the ingredients.
3. Customize (optional): Add a pinch of ground cinnamon for a warm flavor or a little sea salt for a savory touch. Adjust the sweetness level by adding more or less dried cranberries.
4. Store: Transfer the mix to an airtight container and store in a cool, dry place for up to a week.

Nutritional Information: Calories: 180-200, Fat: 10-15g, Carbohydrates: 5-10g, Protein: 5-10g, Fiber: 3-5g, Sodium: 100mg

Tips:
- Use unsalted nuts and seeds whenever possible to control sodium intake.
- Substitute other nuts and seeds based on your preferences and dietary restrictions. Consider macadamia nuts, cashews, chia seeds, or hemp seeds.
- Portion out individual servings into small bags or containers for convenient snacking on the go.
- Pair this mix with sliced vegetables, low-fat yogurt, or unsweetened dark chocolate for a more satisfying snack.
- Consult a registered dietitian or healthcare professional for personalized advice on managing your diabetes through diet and healthy snacking.

Cheese and Whole Grain Crackers

Prep Time: 5 minutes | **Cooking Time**: N/A | **Total Time**: 5 minutes | **Serving Size**: 1 person

Ingredients:

- 2-3 whole-grain crackers (look for crackers with at least 3g fiber per serving)
- 1 ounce low-fat or fat-free cheese (mozzarella, ricotta, cottage cheese, string cheese)
- Optional toppings: sliced vegetables (cucumber, tomato, and bell pepper), fresh herbs (basil, parsley), fruit spread (unsweetened applesauce, mashed berries)

Directions:

1. Wash and prepare any optional toppings you'd like to use.
2. Choose your whole-grain crackers. Look for options with at least 3g fiber per serving and check the sodium content (aim for lower sodium options).
3. Slice or portion your cheese to fit the crackers.
4. Arrange the cheese on the crackers.
5. Add your desired toppings (optional).

Nutritional Information: Calories: 150-200, Carbohydrates: 15-20g, Protein: 8-10g, Fat: 5-7g, Fiber: 2-3g, Sodium: Varies depending on cheese

Tips:

- For a sweeter treat, spread unsweetened applesauce or mashed berries on the crackers before adding cheese.
- Experiment with different cheese and cracker combinations to find your favorites.
- Pair your snack with a glass of water or unsweetened tea for added hydration.
- Portion control is key! Stick to the recommended serving size to manage your carbohydrate intake.
- Consider individual preferences and dietary restrictions when choosing cheese and crackers.
- Consult your doctor or a registered dietitian for personalized dietary advice for managing diabetes.

Apple Slices with Peanut Butter

Prep Time: 5 minutes | **Cooking Time**: N/A | **Total Time**: 5 minutes | **Serving Size**: 1

Ingredients:

- 1 medium apple (choose a variety with a lower glycemic index, like Granny Smith or Gala)
- 2 tablespoons natural peanut butter (unsweetened and without added sugar)
- 1/4 teaspoon cinnamon (optional)
- Optional toppings: Sliced almonds, chia seeds, or a sprinkle of unsweetened cocoa powder

Directions:

1. Wash and prepare the apple: Wash the apple thoroughly and remove the core using an apple corer or knife.
2. Slice the apple: Cut the apple into thin slices (about 1/4 inch thick) or bite-sized chunks.
3. Spread the peanut butter: Spread 1 tablespoon of peanut butter on a plate or small bowl.
4. Dip or spread: Dip the apple slices in the peanut butter or spread a thin layer of the remaining 1 tablespoon onto the slices.
5. Season (optional): Sprinkle with cinnamon for added flavor and warmth.
6. Add toppings (optional): Top with a sprinkle of sliced almonds, chia seeds, or unsweetened cocoa powder for extra crunch and nutrients.

Nutritional Information: Calories: 190, Carbohydrates: 25g, Fiber: 4g, Sugar: 18g, Fat: 8g, Protein: 3g

Tips:

- Use a portion control container to measure out one serving of apple slices and two tablespoons of peanut butter.
- Choose ripe but firm apples for optimal crunch and texture.
- If you prefer a thinner peanut butter consistency, mix a small amount of water or unsweetened almond milk until desired texture is reached.
- Substitute other nut butters like almond butter or sunflower seed butter if you have peanut allergies.
- Pair this snack with unsweetened green tea or water for a complete and satisfying mini-meal.

Cottage Cheese with Pineapple

Prep Time: 5 Minutes | **Cooking Time**: 0 Minutes | **Total Time**: 5 Minutes | **Serving Size**: 1

Ingredients:

- 1/2 cup low-fat cottage cheese
- 1/4 cup fresh pineapple, chopped
- 1/4 teaspoon ground cinnamon (optional)
- 1 tablespoon chopped nuts or seeds (optional)
- 1/2 teaspoon unsweetened shredded coconut (optional)
- Drizzle of sugar-free maple syrup or honey (optional)

Directions:

1. Combine the cottage cheese and pineapple in a small bowl. You can enjoy it as is, or add your desired toppings.
2. For additional flavor and texture, sprinkle with cinnamon, nuts, seeds, or coconut. Choose one or combine them for a burst of taste and crunch.
3. If you prefer a sweeter taste, drizzle a small amount of sugar-free maple syrup or honey on top. Be mindful of portion control, as even sugar-free sweeteners can impact blood sugar levels.

Nutritional Information: Calories: 140, Carbohydrates: 18g, Sugars: 13g, Protein: 14g, Fat: 3g, Fiber: 1g, Sodium: 180mg

Tips:

- Use full-fat cottage cheese if you need more calories or prefer a creamier texture. Just be aware that it will increase the fat content.
- For a richer flavor, use canned pineapple in its own juice (drained) instead of fresh.
- If you're concerned about sodium, choose low-sodium cottage cheese.
- Add a scoop of unsweetened protein powder for an extra protein boost.
- Experiment with different fruits like berries, melon, or grapes.
- Enjoy this snack chilled for a refreshing treat.

Yogurt Parfait

Prep Time: 5 minutes | **Cooking Time**: 0 minutes | **Total Time**: 5 minutes | **Serving Size**: 1

Ingredients:

- 1/2 cup plain Greek yogurt (unsweetened or low-sugar)
- 1/4 cup berries (fresh or frozen)
- 1/4 cup sliced almonds or walnuts
- 1 tablespoon chia seeds
- 1/4 teaspoon ground cinnamon
- Optional: 1 tablespoon unsweetened shredded coconut

Directions:

1. In a small bowl or parfait glass, layer half of the Greek yogurt.
2. Top with half of the berries.
3. Sprinkle with half of the almonds or walnuts and half of the chia seeds.
4. Repeat layers with remaining yogurt, berries, nuts, and chia seeds.
5. Sprinkle with ground cinnamon and optional shredded coconut.
6. Enjoy immediately or refrigerate for up to 2 hours.

Nutritional Information: Calories: 250, Carbohydrates: 25g, Protein: 15g, Fat: 5g, Fiber: 5g

Tips:

1. Use unsweetened or low-sugar Greek yogurt to keep the carb content low.
2. Choose berries that are lower in sugar, such as raspberries, blueberries, or blackberries.
3. Swap the nuts for another healthy topping, such as seeds or chopped dark chocolate.
4. Use a sugar substitute, like stevia, to top the parfait if desired.
5. For a thicker parfait, use thicker yogurt or add a sprinkle of psyllium husk powder.
6. Feel free to adjust the ingredients to your liking and preferences.

Cherry Tomatoes with Mozzarella

Prep Time: 5 minutes | **Cooking Time**: N/A | **Total Time**: 5 minutes | **Serving Size**: 1

Ingredients:
- 10-12 cherry tomatoes, halved
- 4-5 mozzarella cheese balls, mini or halved
- 1 tablespoon fresh basil leaves, chopped (optional)
- 1 tablespoon balsamic vinegar (optional)
- 1 tablespoon extra-virgin olive oil
- Salt and pepper to taste
- Toothpicks (optional)

Directions:
1. Wash and halve the cherry tomatoes.
2. If using mini mozzarella balls, leave them whole. If using larger balls, halve them.
3. In a bowl, combine the tomatoes, mozzarella, and basil (if using).
4. Drizzle with olive oil and balsamic vinegar (if using).
5. Season with salt and pepper to taste.
6. Optional: Thread the tomatoes and mozzarella onto toothpicks for a fun presentation.
7. Serve immediately and enjoy

Nutritional Information: Calories: 80, Carbohydrates: 5g, Sugar: 3g, Fiber: 1g, Fat: 4g, Protein: 5g, Sodium: 120mg

Tips:
- For a more flavorful snack, use grape tomatoes instead of cherry tomatoes.
- Add a sprinkle of dried oregano or Italian seasoning for extra flavor.
- If you are watching your sodium intake, use low-sodium mozzarella cheese.
- Enjoy this snack with whole-wheat crackers or slices of cucumber for a more filling option.

Avocado and Whole Grain Toast

Prep Time: 5 minutes | **Cooking Time**: 0 minutes | **Total Time**: 5 minutes | **Serving Size**: 1

Ingredients:

- 1 slice whole wheat bread
- 1/4 avocado, mashed
- Pinch of salt and pepper
- Optional toppings:
- Sliced tomato
- Chopped cucumber
- Fresh herbs (e.g., cilantro, basil)
- Lemon juice
- Reduced-fat feta cheese
- Everything bagel seasoning

Directions:

1. Toast the bread if desired. You can use a toaster, oven, or stovetop griddle.
2. Mash the avocado in a bowl with a fork. Season with salt and pepper to taste.
3. Spread the mashed avocado onto the toasted bread.
4. Top with your chosen toppings. Be mindful of portion sizes for any additional ingredients, especially those higher in carbohydrates or sodium.

Nutritional Information: Calories: 220, Carbohydrates: 24g, Fiber: 6g, Sugar: 2g, Protein: 8g, Fat: 12g, Sodium: 180mg

Tips:

- Choose ripe avocados for the best flavor and texture.
- If you're short on time, you can use pre-mashed avocado.
- For extra protein, add a scrambled egg or smoked salmon on top.
- Experiment with different toppings to find your favorites.
- Remember to consult with your doctor or registered dietitian for personalized advice on managing your diabetes.

BEVERAGES

Cinnamon Tea

Prep Time: 5 minutes | **Cooking Time**: 5 minutes | **Total Time**: 10 minutes | **Serving Size**: 1

Ingredients:
- 1 cinnamon stick
- 1 cup boiling water

Directions:
1. Add the cinnamon stick to a mug.
2. Pour boiling water over the cinnamon stick.
3. Steep for 5-10 minutes, depending on desired strength.
4. Remove the cinnamon stick and enjoy warm.

Nutritional Information: Calories: 2, Carbohydrates: 0.1g, Sugar: 0g, Fat: 0g, Protein: 0g, Fiber: 0g, Sodium: 0mg

Tips:
- For a sweeter taste, add a natural sweetener like stevia or monk fruit extract after consulting your healthcare professional.
- You can also add other spices like ginger or cardamom for additional flavor and potential health benefits.

Hibiscus Tea

Prep Time: 5 minutes | **Cooking Time**: 5 minutes | **Total Time**: 10 minutes | **Serving Size**: 1

Ingredients:
- 2 hibiscus tea bags or 1 tablespoon dried hibiscus flowers
- 1 cup boiling water

Directions:
1. Place the hibiscus tea bags or flowers in a mug.
2. Pour boiling water over the hibiscus.
3. Steep for 5-10 minutes, depending on desired strength.
4. Remove the tea bags or flowers and enjoy warm or chilled.

Nutritional Information: Calories: 1, Carbohydrates: 0.1g, Sugar: 0g, Fat: 0g, Protein: 0g, Fiber: 0g, Sodium: 0mg

Tips:
- Hibiscus tea can be tart, so you can add a natural sweetener like stevia or monk fruit extract after consulting your healthcare professional.
- You can also add a squeeze of lemon or lime for additional flavor and vitamin C.

Green Tea

Prep Time: 5 minutes | **Cooking Time**: 0 minutes | **Total Time**: 5 minutes | **Serving Size**: 1

Ingredients:
- 1 cup hot water
- 1 green tea bag or 1 tsp. loose leaf green tea
- Optional:
- Fresh or frozen fruit (berries, citrus slices, etc.)
- Herbs and spices (ginger, mint, cinnamon, etc.)
- Sugar-free sweetener (stevia, erythritol, etc.) - use sparingly and consider alternatives like fruit for sweetness

Directions:
1. Heat water to desired temperature (around 175°F for most green teas).
2. Steep tea bag or loose leaf tea according to package instructions. Remove tea bag or strain loose leaf tea.
3. Add optional ingredients like fruit, herbs, and sweetener to taste.
4. Enjoy hot or cold.

Nutritional Information: Calories: 1, Carbohydrates: 0.1g, Sugar: 0g, Fat: 0g, Protein: 0g, Fiber: 0g, Sodium: 0mg

Tips:
- Experiment with different flavor combinations to find your favorites.
- Use unsweetened fruit or sugar-free alternatives to avoid added sugar.
- Be mindful of the caffeine content in green tea, especially if you are sensitive to caffeine.

Green Power Juice

Prep Time: 5 minutes | **Total Time**: 5 minutes | **Serving Size**: 1 glass

Nutritional information: Calories: 50, Carbs: 5g, Fiber: 2g, Sugar: 3g, Vitamins A, C, K, Folate

Ingredients:
- 1 handful spinach
- 1 cucumber
- 1 celery stalk
- 1/2 green bell pepper
- 1/4 lemon (optional)
- Water
- to adjust consistency

Directions:
Wash and chop all ingredients. Juice them together in a juicer. Add water for desired consistency.

Berry Protein Smoothie with Unsweetened Soy Milk

Prep Time: 5 minutes | **Cooking Time**: N/A | **Total Time**: 5 minutes | **Servings**: 1

Ingredients:

- 1 cup unsweetened soy milk
- 1/2 cup frozen berries (mixed, blueberries, etc.)
- 1/2 scoop unflavored protein powder
- 1/4 cup spinach
- 1/2 cup ice
- Optional: Stevia to taste

Directions:

1. Blend all ingredients until smooth and creamy.
2. Adjust sweetness with stevia if desired.

Nutritional Information: Calories: 200, Carbs: 20g, Protein: 20g, Fat: 4g

Turmeric Ginger Latte with Unsweetened Coconut Milk

Prep Time: 5 minutes | **Cooking Time**: 5 minutes | **Total Time**: 10 minutes | **Servings**: 1

Ingredients:

- 1 cup unsweetened coconut milk
- 1/2 cup water
- 1/2 inch turmeric root, peeled and grated
- 1/2 inch ginger root, peeled and grated
- 1/4 teaspoon black pepper
- Optional: Stevia to taste

Directions:

1. Combine all ingredients in a saucepan.
2. Heat over medium heat, bringing to a simmer, and let steep for 5 minutes.
3. Strain and enjoy hot or cold.

Nutritional Information: Calories: 30, Carbs: 5g, Protein: 0g, Fat: 4g

Simple Coconut Water

Prep Time: 5 minutes | **Cooking Time**: N/A | **Total Time**: 5 minutes | **Serving Size**: 1 cup

Nutritional Information: Calories: 45, Carbs: 9g, Sugar: 6g, Fiber: 0g, Potassium: 45mg

Ingredients:

- 1 cup unsweetened coconut water
- Optional: Squeeze of lime juice, pinch of sea salt

Directions:

1. Pour coconut water into a glass.
2. Add lime juice and salt to taste, if desired.
3. Serve chilled.

Spiced Coconut Water

Prep Time: 5 minutes | **Cooking Time**: N/A | **Total Time**: 5 minutes | **Serving Size**: 1 cup

Nutritional Information: Calories: 45-60, Carbs: 9-12g, Sugar: 6-8g, Fiber: 0g, Potassium: 45mg

Ingredients:

- 1 cup unsweetened coconut water
- 1/4 teaspoon ground cinnamon
- Pinch of ground ginger
- Pinch of ground nutmeg
- Optional: Dash of cayenne pepper (for a kick)

Directions:

1. Pour coconut water into a glass.
2. Add spices to taste and stir well.
3. Serve chilled.

Coconut Water Smoothie

Prep Time: 5 minutes | **Cooking Time**: N/A | **Total Time**: 5 minutes | **Serving Size**: 1 cup

Nutritional Information: Calories: 80-150, Carbs: 15-25g, Sugar: 8-15g, Fiber: 2-5g, Potassium: 45mg

Ingredients:

- 1 cup unsweetened coconut water
- 1/2 cup frozen spinach
- 1/4 avocado
- 1/2 cucumber, peeled and chopped
- 1/4 cup fresh berries
- Optional: Squeeze of lime juice, pinch of chia seeds

Directions:

1. Blend all ingredients in a blender until smooth.
2. Add lime juice and chia seeds to taste, if desired.
3. Serve chilled.

Sparkling Coconut Water

Prep Time: 5 minutes | **Cooking Time**: N/A | **Total Time**: 5 minutes | **Serving Size**: 1 cup

Nutritional Information: Calories: 45-70, Carbs: 9-13g, Sugar: 6-9g, Fiber: 0g, Potassium: 45mg

Ingredients:

- 1 cup unsweetened coconut water
- 1/4 cup club soda
- Fresh herbs like mint or basil, for garnish
- Optional: Squeeze of lime juice

Directions:

- Pour coconut water and club soda into a glass.
- Garnish with herbs and lime juice to taste.
- Serve chilled.

DESERT

Fruit Salad with Mint

Prep Time: 10 minutes | **Cooking Time**: 0 minutes | **Total Time**: 10 minutes **Serving Size**: 2-3

Ingredients:
- 1 cup mixed berries (fresh or frozen)
- 1/2 cup diced melon (cantaloupe, honeydew, or watermelon)
- 1/2 cup diced apple (with skin for added fiber)
- 1/4 cup diced pear
- 1/4 cup grapes, halved
- 1/4 cup mandarin oranges, segmented
- 1/4 cup chopped fresh mint
- 1/4 cup plain Greek yogurt (unsweetened)
- 1 tablespoon lemon juice
- 1/2 teaspoon cinnamon (optional)
- Stevia or sugar substitute to taste (optional)

Directions:
1. Wash and prepare all fruits. Remove any stems, pits, or seeds. Dice or segment the fruits into bite-sized pieces.
2. Combine the fruits in a large bowl. Gently toss them together to mix.
3. In a separate small bowl, whisk together the Greek yogurt, lemon juice, cinnamon (if using), and sweetener (if using). Adjust the amount of sweetener to your taste preference.
4. Pour the yogurt dressing over the fruit salad. Gently fold it in to coat the fruits evenly.
5. Sprinkle the chopped mint over the salad. Serve immediately or chill for a few minutes for a colder dessert.

Nutritional Information: Calories: 120, Carbohydrates: 20g, Fiber: 5g, Sugar: 15g, Fat: 0g, Protein: 1g

Tips:
- For a richer flavor, use a flavored Greek yogurt, such as vanilla or lemon.
- If you don't have fresh mint, you can use 1/4 teaspoon dried mint instead.
- You can substitute other fruits for the ones listed in the recipe, based on your preferences and what's in season. Just be sure to choose fruits that are lower in sugar, such as berries, melons, and citrus fruits.
- If you have a blender or food processor, you can puree a small portion of the berries or other fruits to create a thicker sauce for the salad.
- This salad is best enjoyed fresh, but you can store any leftovers in an airtight container in the refrigerator for up to 2 days.

Baked Pears with Cinnamon and Walnuts

Prep Time: 10 minutes | **Cooking Time**: 25 minutes | **Total Time**: 35 minutes | **Serving Size**: 2

Ingredients:
- 2 ripe but firm pears (such as Bartlett or Bosc)
- 1/2 teaspoon ground cinnamon
- 1/4 cup chopped walnuts, toasted (optional)
- 1 tablespoon unsweetened nut butter (such as almond or peanut butter)
- 1/4 teaspoon vanilla extract
- 1/4 cup unsweetened applesauce
- 1/4 teaspoon ground ginger (optional)
- Pinch of nutmeg (optional)
- 1 tablespoon fresh lemon juice (optional)

Directions:
1. Preheat oven to 375°F (190°C). Lightly grease a baking dish.
2. Wash and dry the pears. Cut them in half lengthwise and core them using a melon baller or spoon.
3. In a small bowl, combine cinnamon, walnuts (if using), nut butter, vanilla extract, applesauce, ginger (if using), nutmeg (if using), and lemon juice (if using).
4. Fill the cavities of the pear halves with the nut butter mixture.
5. Place the pears in the prepared baking dish, cut side up.
6. Bake for 25-30 minutes, or until the pears are tender and slightly golden brown.
7. Let the pears cool slightly before serving.

Nutritional Information: Calories: 160 Carbohydrates: 24g, Sugars: 18g, Fiber: 6g, Fat: 5g, Protein: 2g

Tips:
- For a more decadent dessert, serve the baked pears with a dollop of low-fat Greek yogurt or ricotta cheese.
- You can also add a sprinkle of sugar-free chocolate chips or chopped dried fruit to the filling.
- To make this recipe vegan, use a dairy-free nut butter and vegan yogurt.
- If you don't have any nut butter, you can substitute it with mashed avocado or ricotta cheese.
- Be sure to choose ripe but firm pears for this recipe. Pears that are too soft will become mushy when baked.

Dark Chocolate-Dipped Banana Slices

Prep Time: 10 minutes | **Cooking Time**: N/A | Total Time: 10 minutes | Serving Size: 10-12

Ingredients:
- 2 ripe bananas, peeled and sliced 1/4-inch thick
- 1/2 cup dark chocolate chips (at least 70% cocoa)
- 1 tablespoon coconut oil, melted (optional)
- Pinch of sea salt (optional)
- Toppings (optional): chopped nuts, shredded coconut, unsweetened cocoa powder

Directions:
1. Freeze the bananas: Place the banana slices on a parchment-lined baking sheet and freeze for at least 2 hours, or until solid.
2. Melt the chocolate: In a microwave-safe bowl, heat the chocolate chips and coconut oil (if using) in 30-second intervals, stirring after each interval, until melted and smooth. Be careful not to overheat, as this can cause the chocolate to seize.
3. Dip the bananas: Using a fork or toothpick, dip each frozen banana slice into the melted chocolate, coating it evenly. Allow excess chocolate to drip off before placing the slice back on the baking sheet.
4. Add toppings (optional): Immediately after dipping, sprinkle with your desired toppings, such as chopped nuts, shredded coconut, or unsweetened cocoa powder.
5. Freeze again: Freeze the chocolate-dipped banana slices for another 30 minutes, or until the chocolate is set.
6. Serve: Enjoy immediately or store in an airtight container in the freezer for up to 2 weeks.

Nutritional Information: Calories: 80, Carbohydrates: 15g, Fiber: 1g, Sugar: 9g, Fat: 3g, Protein: 1g

Tips:
- For a richer chocolate flavor, use dark chocolate with a higher cocoa content (up to 85%).
- If you don't have coconut oil, you can use vegetable oil instead.
- To make the slices even more diabetic-friendly, drizzle them with a small amount of sugar-free chocolate syrup instead of using chocolate chips.
- Let the bananas thaw slightly before dipping them in the chocolate, as this will help the chocolate adhere better.
- Be sure to use ripe but firm bananas, as mushy bananas will be difficult to dip and freeze.

Chia Seed Pudding Parfait

Prep Time: 5 minutes | **Cooking Time**: N/A | **Total Time**: 5 minutes | **Serving Size**: 1

Ingredients:

- 1/4 cup chia seeds
- 1 cup unsweetened almond milk (or other low-carb milk alternative)
- 1/4 teaspoon vanilla extract
- 1/4 teaspoon ground cinnamon
- 1/4 cup plain Greek yogurt
- 1/4 cup mixed berries (fresh or frozen)
- 1/4 cup chopped nuts (almonds, walnuts, pecans)
- Optional: Sugar substitute to taste

Directions:

1. Make the chia pudding: In a small bowl, whisk together chia seeds, almond milk, vanilla extract, and cinnamon. Cover and refrigerate for at least 2 hours, or overnight, until thickened. Stir occasionally to prevent clumps.
2. Assemble the parfait: In a serving glass, layer half of the chia pudding. Top with half of the Greek yogurt and half of the berries. Repeat with another layer of chia pudding, yogurt, and berries.
3. Sprinkle with chopped nuts and optional sugar substitute if desired.
4. Serve immediately or chill for another 30 minutes for a thicker consistency.

Nutritional Information: Calories: 250, Carbohydrates: 20g, Fiber: 8g, Protein: 8g, Fat: 7g

Tips:

- For a richer flavor, use full-fat Greek yogurt.
- Add a tablespoon of unsweetened cocoa powder to the chia pudding for a chocolatey twist.
- Substitute other low-carb fruits like raspberries, blackberries, or sliced kiwi.
- Experiment with different spices like nutmeg, ginger, or cardamom.
- Use chia seeds ground into a flour for an even smoother pudding texture.
- This parfait can be made ahead of time and stored in the refrigerator for up to 3 days.

Frozen Yogurt Bark

Prep Time: 5 minutes | **Cooking Time**: 0 minutes | **Total Time**: 5 minutes | **Serving Size**: 4-6

Ingredients:

- 1 cup plain Greek yogurt (unsweetened or low-sugar)
- 1/4 cup berries (fresh or frozen), chopped
- 1/4 cup nuts and seeds (chopped almonds, pistachios, pumpkin seeds, etc.)
- 1 tablespoon unsweetened cocoa powder (optional)
- 1 tablespoon sugar-free maple syrup or stevia (optional)
- 1/4 teaspoon vanilla extract

Directions:

1. Prepare the pan: Line a baking sheet with parchment paper.
2. Mix the yogurt: In a bowl, whisk together the Greek yogurt, vanilla extract, and optional sweetener. If using cocoa powder, whisk it in until evenly incorporated.
3. Spread the yogurt: Pour the yogurt mixture onto the prepared baking sheet and spread it evenly into a thin layer.
4. Add toppings: Sprinkle the chopped berries, nuts, and seeds on top of the yogurt layer.
5. Freeze: Place the baking sheet in the freezer and let it set for at least 3 hours, or until completely frozen solid.
6. Break and serve: Once frozen, remove the baking sheet from the freezer and break the bark into pieces. Enjoy immediately

Nutritional Information: Calories: 150-200, Carbohydrates: 15-20g, Protein: 10-15g, Fat: 5-10g

Tips:

- Use sugar-free sweeteners like stevia or monk fruit to keep the sugar content low.
- Experiment with different fruit and nut combinations.
- For a richer flavor, use full-fat Greek yogurt. However, be mindful of the increased calorie content.
- Top with a drizzle of melted sugar-free chocolate for an extra treat.
- Store leftover bark in the freezer in an airtight container for up to a week.

Coconut and Almond Energy Bites

Prep Time: 10 minutes | **Cooking Time**: None | **Total Time**: 10 minutes | **Serving Size**: 10-12

Ingredients:

- 1/2 cup unsweetened shredded coconut
- 1/2 cup rolled oats
- 1/4 cup almond butter
- 1/4 cup chopped unsweetened Medjool dates
- 1/4 cup unsweetened almond milk
- 1 tablespoon chia seeds
- 1/4 teaspoon ground cinnamon
- Pinch of sea salt

Directions:

1. In a large bowl, combine the shredded coconut, rolled oats, almond butter, chopped dates, almond milk, chia seeds, cinnamon, and salt. Mix well until everything is evenly combined and forms a sticky dough.
2. Using a spoon or your hands, roll the dough into 1-inch balls. Place the balls on a baking sheet lined with parchment paper.
3. Refrigerate for at least 30 minutes, or until firm. This allows the flavors to meld and the chia seeds to activate.

Nutritional Information: Calories: 180, Carbohydrates: 12g, Fiber: 4g, Protein: 6g, Fat: 12g

Tips:

- For a more decadent flavor, drizzle the bites with melted dark chocolate (choose one with at least 70% cocoa).
- Substitute other nut butters like peanut butter or cashew butter for almond butter.
- Add a tablespoon of chopped dried fruit like cranberries or cherries for extra sweetness and texture.
- If the mixture is too dry, add a little more almond milk, one tablespoon at a time, until it reaches the desired consistency.
- Store leftover bites in an airtight container in the refrigerator for up to 5 days.

Baked Cinnamon Apple Slices

Prep Time: 10 minutes | **Cooking Time**: 30-35 minutes | **Total Time**: 40-45 minutes | **Serving Size**: 4

Ingredients:

- 2 medium apples (such as Granny Smith, Fuji, or Honeycrisp), cored and thinly sliced (about 1/4 inch thick)
- 1 tablespoon lemon juice
- 1/4 cup unsweetened applesauce
- 1/2 teaspoon ground cinnamon
- 1/4 teaspoon ground nutmeg
- 1/8 teaspoon ground ginger
- 1/4 teaspoon ground cloves
- 1/8 teaspoon salt
- Optional toppings: Chopped nuts, whipped cream, Greek yogurt

Directions:

1. Preheat oven to 375°F (190°C). Line a baking sheet with parchment paper.
2. In a large bowl, toss the apple slices with lemon juice to prevent browning.
3. In a separate bowl, whisk together applesauce, cinnamon, nutmeg, ginger, cloves, and salt.
4. Coat the apple slices with the spice mixture, making sure they are evenly coated.
5. Arrange the apple slices in a single layer on the prepared baking sheet.
6. Bake for 30-35 minutes, or until the apples are tender and slightly golden brown.
7. Let cool slightly before serving.
8. Enjoy as is or top with your desired toppings.

Nutritional Information: Calories: 80, Carbohydrates: 18g, Fiber: 4g, Sugar: 10g, Fat: 2g, Protein: 0.5g

Tips:

- For a sweeter option, you can sprinkle a small amount of granulated sugar substitute over the apples before baking.
- You can also use other spices like cardamom or allspice in this recipe.
- If you don't have applesauce, you can use mashed banana or another unsweetened fruit puree.
- Be sure to monitor your blood sugar levels after eating this dessert, as it does contain natural sugars from the apples.

Homemade Berry Sorbet

Prep Time: 5 minutes | **Cooking Time**: None | **Total Time**: 5 minutes | **Servings**: 4

Ingredients:

- 2 cups frozen mixed berries (such as strawberries, raspberries, blueberries)
- 1/4 cup water
- 1 tablespoon lemon juice (optional)
- 1/2 teaspoon stevia powder (optional, or to taste)
- Fresh mint leaves for garnish (optional)

Directions:

1. Prepare the berries: If using fresh berries, freeze them for at least 2 hours before making the sorbet.
2. Blend the ingredients: In a blender, combine the frozen berries, water, lemon juice (if using), and stevia (if using). Blend until smooth.
3. Taste and adjust: If the sorbet is too tart, add more stevia to taste. If it's too thick, add a little more water.
4. Freeze: Pour the sorbet into a freezer-safe container and freeze for at least 3 hours, or until firm.
5. Serve: Scoop the sorbet into bowls and garnish with fresh mint leaves, if desired.

Nutritional Information: Calories: 80, Carbohydrates: 15g, Sugar: 5g, Fat: 0g, Protein: 1g, Fiber: 3g

Tips:

- You can use any type of frozen berries you like.
- For a richer flavor, use unsweetened frozen yogurt instead of water.
- If you don't have a blender, you can use a food processor.
- To make the sorbet ahead of time, freeze it for up to 2 weeks.
- Be mindful of portion sizes, as even healthy treats should be enjoyed in moderation.

Avocado Chocolate Mousse

Prep Time: 5 minutes | **Cooking Time**: N/A | **Total Time**: 5 minutes | **Serving Size**: 2

Ingredients:

- 1 ripe avocado, peeled and pitted
- 2 tablespoons unsweetened cocoa powder
- 1/4 cup unsweetened almond milk
- 1 tablespoon maple syrup (or other sugar substitute to taste)
- 1/2 teaspoon vanilla extract
- Pinch of salt
- Optional Toppings:
- Fresh berries (raspberries, blueberries, strawberries)
- Chopped nuts (almonds, pecans, walnuts)
- Unsweetened shredded coconut

Directions:

1. Combine all ingredients: In a food processor or blender, combine the avocado, cocoa powder, almond milk, maple syrup, vanilla extract, and salt.
2. Blend until smooth: Blend until the mixture is completely smooth and creamy, scraping down the sides as needed. You may need to add a little more almond milk if the mixture is too thick.
3. Chill and serve: Divide the mousse between two serving bowls and chill in the refrigerator for at least 30 minutes. This will allow the flavors to meld and the mousse to thicken up.
4. Top and enjoy: Garnish the mousse with your desired toppings.

Nutritional Information: Calories: 220, Carbohydrates: 15g (including 7g fiber) Sugar: 5g, Fat: 18g, Protein: 4g

Tips:

- For an extra rich chocolate flavor, use dark cocoa powder.
- If you don't have maple syrup, you can use another sugar substitute to taste.
- You can add a scoop of your favorite protein powder for an extra boost of protein.
- This mousse is best served immediately after chilling, but it can also be stored in the refrigerator for up to 24 hours.

Yogurt Parfait with Granola

Prep Time: 5 minutes | **Cooking Time**: 0 minutes | **Total Time**: 5 minutes | **Serving Size**: 1

Ingredients:

- 1 cup plain Greek yogurt, unsweetened
- 1/2 cup mixed berries (fresh or frozen)
- 1/4 cup granola, low-sugar or sugar-free
- 1/4 cup chopped nuts (walnuts, almonds, pecans)
- 1/2 teaspoon ground cinnamon
- Optional: 1 tablespoon sliced strawberries or other fresh fruit for garnish

Directions:

1. In a bowl, combine the Greek yogurt and cinnamon. Stir well to combine.
2. Divide the yogurt mixture evenly between two small glasses or parfaits cups.
3. Top each yogurt layer with half of the mixed berries.
4. Sprinkle half of the granola and half of the chopped nuts over the berries.
5. Repeat layers with the remaining yogurt, berries, granola, and nuts.
6. Garnish with optional sliced strawberries or other fresh fruit.
7. Serve immediately or chill for a few minutes before enjoying.

Nutritional Information: Calories: 300, Carbohydrates: 30g, Fiber: 8g, Protein: 20g, Fat: 5g, Sugar: 10g

Tips:

- Use unsweetened or low-sugar yogurt to keep the sugar content low.
- Choose a granola that is low in sugar and high in fiber. Look for ones with nuts, seeds, and whole grains.
- Add a sprinkle of chia seeds for extra protein and fiber.
- Top with a drizzle of low-sugar maple syrup or honey, if desired.
- Experiment with different fruits, nuts, and spices to find your favorite combinations.
- If you're using frozen berries, let them thaw slightly before adding them to the parfait.
- Make this parfait ahead of time and store it in the refrigerator for up to 2 days.

SALAD

Classic Greek Salad

Prep Time: 10 minutes | **Cooking Time**: 0 minutes | **Total Time**: 10 minutes **Serving Size**: 1

Ingredients:
- 1 cup romaine lettuce, chopped
- 1/2 cucumber, sliced
- 1/2 red bell pepper, sliced
- 1/4 red onion, thinly sliced
- 1/4 cup cherry tomatoes, halved
- 1/4 cup crumbled feta cheese
- 10 Kalamata olives, pitted and halved
- 2 tablespoons extra virgin olive oil
- 1 tablespoon lemon juice
- 1/2 teaspoon dried oregano
- 1/4 teaspoon salt
- 1/4 teaspoon black pepper

Directions:
1. Wash and prepare vegetables: Rinse the romaine lettuce and tear into bite-sized pieces. Wash and slice the cucumber, bell pepper, and red onion. Halve the cherry tomatoes. Pit and halve the Kalamata olives.
2. Assemble the salad: In a large bowl, combine the chopped romaine lettuce, cucumber, bell pepper, red onion, and cherry tomatoes.
3. Add cheese and olives: Top the salad with crumbled feta cheese and halved Kalamata olives.
4. Make the dressing: In a small bowl, whisk together the olive oil, lemon juice, dried oregano, salt, and black pepper.
5. Dress the salad: Drizzle the prepared dressing over the salad and toss gently to coat all ingredients evenly.Serve immediately

Nutritional Information: Calories: 230, Carbohydrates: 12g, Net carbs: 8g, Fiber: 4g, Fat: 14g, Protein: 8g

Tips
- Portion control: Stick to the recommended serving size to manage your carbohydrate intake.
- Choose lean protein: Add a grilled chicken breast or shrimp to the salad for extra protein and satiety.
- Go light on the dressing: Use a moderate amount of dressing to control fat and added sugar.
- Substitute feta: Opt for low-fat feta cheese to reduce saturated fat intake.
- Add healthy carbs: Incorporate a small amount of quinoa or whole-wheat croutons for additional fiber and nutrients.

Quinoa and Vegetable Salad

Prep Time: 15 minutes | **Cooking Time**: 15 minutes | **Total Time**: 30 minutes | **Serving Size**: 2-3

Ingredients:
- 1 cup uncooked quinoa, rinsed
- 1 ½ cups water or vegetable broth
- ½ cup chopped cucumber
- ½ cup chopped cherry tomatoes
- ¼ cup chopped red onion
- ¼ cup crumbled feta cheese (optional, for non-vegans)
- ¼ cup chopped fresh parsley
- 1 tablespoon olive oil
- 2 tablespoons lemon juice
- ½ teaspoon dried oregano
- Salt and pepper to taste

Directions:
1. Cook the quinoa: In a saucepan, combine quinoa and water or broth. Bring to a boil, then reduce heat, cover, and simmer for 15 minutes, or until quinoa is fluffy and cooked through. Fluff with a fork and set aside to cool slightly.
2. Prepare the vegetables: While the quinoa cooks, chop the cucumber, tomatoes, red onion, and parsley.
3. Assemble the salad: In a large bowl, combine the cooled quinoa, chopped vegetables, and feta cheese (if using).
4. Make the dressing: In a small bowl, whisk together olive oil, lemon juice, oregano, salt, and pepper.
5. Dress the salad: Pour the dressing over the salad and toss gently to coat all ingredients.
6. Serve: Garnish with fresh parsley and enjoy immediately

Nutritional Information: Calories: 350, Carbohydrates: 35g, Fiber: 5g, Protein: 10g, Fat: 15g

Tips:
- For added flavor and protein, roast the vegetables before adding them to the salad.
- Substitute crumbled tofu or chickpeas for the feta cheese for a vegan option.
- Use low-sodium feta cheese or omit it altogether to reduce sodium content.
- Feel free to customize the vegetables based on your preferences. Other options include bell peppers, carrots, celery, or zucchini.
- Store leftover salad in an airtight container in the refrigerator for up to 3 days.

Chicken Caesar Salad

Prep Time: 10 minutes | **Cooking Time**: 20 minutes | **Total Time**: 30 minutes | **Servings**: 2

Ingredients:
Salad:
- 2 cups romaine lettuce, chopped
- 1/2 cup grilled or baked chicken breast, sliced
- 1/4 cup cherry tomatoes, halved
- 1/4 cup cucumber, sliced
- 1/4 red onion, thinly sliced (optional)
- 1/4 cup crumbled feta cheese (optional)

Dressing:
- 3 tablespoons plain Greek yogurt
- 1 tablespoon olive oil
- 1 tablespoon lemon juice
- 1 teaspoon Dijon mustard
- 1/2 teaspoon Worcestershire sauce
- 1/4 teaspoon garlic powder
- Pinch of black pepper
- Dash of red pepper flakes (optional)

Toppings:
- 1/4 cup whole-wheat croutons (optional)
- 1 tablespoon grated Parmesan cheese

Directions:
1. Prepare the dressing: In a small bowl, whisk together Greek yogurt, olive oil, lemon juice, Dijon mustard, Worcestershire sauce, garlic powder, pepper, and red pepper flakes (if using).
2. Cook the chicken: Grill or bake your chicken breast until cooked through. Slice or cube the chicken.
3. Assemble the salad: In a large bowl, combine the romaine lettuce, chicken, tomatoes, cucumber, red onion (if using), and feta cheese (if using).
4. Drizzle with dressing: Toss the salad with enough dressing to coat evenly. You can reserve some dressing on the side for individual preference.
5. Top and serve: Garnish with whole-wheat croutons (if using) and Parmesan cheese.

Nutritional Information: Calories: 350, Carbohydrates: 20g, Protein: 30g, Fat: 15g, Fiber: 4g, Sodium: 300mg

Tips
- Use lean protein sources like grilled or baked chicken breast.
- Limit high-carbohydrate ingredients like croutons. Use a smaller amount or opt for whole-wheat alternatives.
- Choose a light Caesar dressing or make your own with healthy ingredients like Greek yogurt and olive oil.
- Add non-starchy vegetables for additional fiber and nutrients.
- Consider adding healthy fats like avocado or nuts for satiety and flavor.
- Pay attention to portion sizes and sodium content in ingredients.

Mango Avocado Salad

Prep Time: 10 minutes | **Cooking Time**: N/A | **Total Time**: 10 minutes | **Serving Size**: 1

Ingredients:

- 1/2 cup mixed greens (spinach, romaine, arugula, etc.)
- 1/2 mango, peeled, pitted, and diced
- 1/2 avocado, peeled, pitted, and sliced
- 1/4 cup crumbled feta cheese (optional)
- 1/4 cup chopped walnuts or pecans
- 1 tablespoon olive oil
- 1 tablespoon lime juice
- 1/2 teaspoon Dijon mustard
- Salt and pepper to taste

Directions:

1. Wash and dry the greens. Place them in a large bowl.
2. Dice the mango and avocado, adding them to the bowl with the greens.
3. Crumble the feta cheese (if using) and sprinkle over the salad.
4. Add the chopped walnuts or pecans.
5. In a small bowl, whisk together the olive oil, lime juice, Dijon mustard, salt, and pepper.
6. Drizzle the dressing over the salad and toss gently to coat.
7. Serve immediately and enjoy.

Nutritional Information: Calories: 250, Carbohydrates: 20g, Sugar: 6g, Fiber: 8g
Fat: 15g, Protein: 3g

Tips:

- For a more substantial salad, add grilled chicken or shrimp.
- Substitute black beans or chickpeas for the feta cheese for a vegan option.
- Use a low-fat yogurt dressing instead of olive oil for a lighter version.
- Experiment with different types of greens and fruit for variety.
- Be mindful of portion sizes, especially with the fruit and nuts, as they contain carbohydrates.

Caprese Salad

Prep Time: 10 minutes | **Cooking Time**: None | **Total Time**: 10 minutes | **Serving Size**: 1

Ingredients:

- 1 large ripe tomato, sliced
- 4 ounces fresh mozzarella cheese, sliced
- 1/4 cup fresh basil leaves, torn
- 1 tablespoon extra-virgin olive oil
- 1/4 teaspoon balsamic vinegar (optional)
- Salt and freshly ground black pepper, to taste

Directions:

1. Arrange the tomato slices on a plate. Top with mozzarella cheese slices.
2. Scatter the basil leaves over the top.
3. Drizzle with olive oil and balsamic vinegar (if using).
4. Season with salt and pepper to taste.

Nutritional Information: Calories: 234, Fat: 18.9g, Saturated Fat: 6.3g, Cholesterol: 30mg, Sodium: 135mg, Total Carbs: 8.1g, Dietary Fiber: 1.2g, Sugars: 4.5g, Protein: 9.8g

Tips:

- Use low-sodium mozzarella cheese or fresh buffalo mozzarella for a lower sodium option.
- Choose vine-ripened tomatoes for the best flavor and sweetness.
- If you're looking for a heartier salad, add in some whole-wheat bread chunks or grilled chicken breast.
- Experiment with different herbs and spices for a flavor variation, such as oregano, thyme, or garlic powder.
- Enjoy the salad as a light lunch or appetizer.

Asian Sesame Chicken Salad

Prep Time: 15 minutes | **Cooking Time**: 20 minutes | **Total Time**: 35 minutes | **Serving** | Size: 2

Ingredients:

For the Chicken:
- 1 boneless, skinless chicken breast
- 1 tablespoon soy sauce (low-sodium preferred)
- 1 tablespoon rice vinegar
- 1 tablespoon toasted sesame oil
- 1 teaspoon grated ginger
- 1 clove garlic, minced
- Pinch of black pepper

For the Salad:
- 4 cups mixed greens (spinach, romaine, or a blend)
- 1 cup shredded broccoli
- 1/2 cup shredded carrots
- 1/4 cup sliced red bell pepper
- 1/4 cup chopped green onions
- 1/4 cup toasted sesame seeds
- 1/4 cup sliced almonds

For the Dressing:
- 2 tablespoons rice vinegar
- 1 tablespoon soy sauce (low-sodium preferred)
- 1 tablespoon toasted sesame oil
- 1 tablespoon honey (or substitute with a sugar-free sweetener)
- 1 teaspoon Dijon mustard
- 1/2 teaspoon grated ginger
- Pinch of black pepper

Directions:

1. Marinate the chicken: In a bowl, combine soy sauce, rice vinegar, sesame oil, ginger, garlic, and pepper. Add the chicken breast and marinate for at least 15 minutes.
2. Cook the chicken: You can grill, bake, or poach the chicken breast.
3. Grill: Preheat grill to medium-high heat and cook chicken for 5-7 minutes per side, until cooked through.
4. Bake: Preheat oven to 400°F (200°C). Place chicken on a baking sheet and bake for 20-25 minutes, or until cooked through.
5. Poach: Bring a pot of water to a simmer. Add chicken and cook for 15-20 minutes, or until cooked through.
6. Prepare the salad: While the chicken cooks, wash and chop the salad greens, broccoli, carrots, bell pepper, and green onions. Toast the sesame seeds and almonds in a dry pan over medium heat until golden brown.
7. Make the dressing: In a small jar or bowl, whisk together all dressing ingredients.
8. Assemble the salad: Slice or shred the cooked chicken. In a large bowl, combine the salad greens, vegetables, chicken, sesame seeds, and almonds.
9. Toss with dressing: Just before serving, drizzle the dressing over the salad and toss to coat evenly.

Nutritional Information: Calories: 400, Carbohydrates: 30g, Protein: 35g, Fat: 15g, Fiber: 5g, Sodium: 350mg

Tips:
- Use brown rice or quinoa instead of white rice for a more fiber-rich option.
- Add other vegetables you enjoy, such as cucumber, snap peas, or edamame.
- Substitute the chicken with grilled tofu or shrimp for a vegetarian option.
- Adjust the amount of dressing to your liking.
- Store leftover salad in an airtight container in the refrigerator for up to 3 days.

Spinach and Strawberry Salad

Prep Time: 10 minutes **Cooking Time**: 0 minutes | **Total Time**: 10 minutes **Servings**: 2

Ingredients:

- 4 cups baby spinach
- 1 cup fresh strawberries, sliced
- 1/4 cup crumbled feta cheese (optional, choose low-fat for reduced sodium)
- 1/4 cup chopped walnuts or pecans (optional, toasted for extra flavor)
- 1/4 cup red onion, thinly sliced
- 2 tablespoons balsamic vinegar
- 1 tablespoon olive oil
- 1/2 teaspoon Dijon mustard
- 1/4 teaspoon dried thyme
- Pinch of salt and black pepper

Directions:

1. Wash and dry the spinach thoroughly. Place in a large bowl.
2. Slice the strawberries and red onion. Add them to the bowl with the spinach.
3. Top with feta cheese and nuts (if using).
4. Whisk together the balsamic vinegar, olive oil, Dijon mustard, thyme, salt, and pepper in a small bowl.
5. Drizzle the dressing over the salad and toss gently to coat all ingredients.
6. Serve immediately and enjoy.

Nutritional Information: Calories: 150, Carbohydrates: 15g, Fiber: 3g, Sugar: 7g, Fat: 7g, Protein: 3g

Tips:
- For a sweeter salad, drizzle with a small amount of honey or maple syrup (use sparingly and consider the added sugar content).
- Substitute feta cheese with crumbled tofu or vegan cheese for a dairy-free option.
- Add other diabetes-friendly ingredients like blueberries, raspberries, or chopped avocado for increased variety and nutrients.
- Adjust the amount of dressing based on your preference. Remember, moderation is key for managing blood sugar levels.
- Store leftover salad in an airtight container in the refrigerator for up to 24 hours. The quality of the salad may decline after that, especially with the strawberries.

Cobb Salad

Prep Time: 15 minutes | **Cooking Time**: 20 minutes | **Total Time**: 35 minutes | **Servings**: 2

Ingredients:
Greens:
- 2 cups mixed greens (romaine, spinach, kale, etc.)
- 1/2 cup baby arugula

Protein:
- 4 oz. grilled chicken breast, sliced
- 2 hard-boiled eggs, sliced
- 1/4 cup crumbled feta cheese

Vegetables:
- 1/2 avocado, sliced
- 1/2 cucumber, sliced
- 1/2 tomato, diced
- 1/4 red onion, sliced
- 1/4 cup cherry tomatoes, halved

Other:
- 2 slices cooked bacon, crumbled (optional)
- 1/4 cup chopped walnuts or pecans
- Olive oil vinaigrette dressing (homemade or store-bought, low-sugar)

Directions:
1. Prepare the greens: Wash and dry the greens. Arrange them in a large bowl.
2. Cook the chicken: Grill, bake, or pan-fry the chicken breast until cooked through. Let it cool and then slice it.
3. Hard-boil the eggs: Place the eggs in a pot of boiling water and cook for 10 minutes. Let them cool, then peel and slice them.
4. Assemble the salad: Layer the greens, chicken, eggs, avocado, cucumber, tomato, red onion, cherry tomatoes, feta cheese, and bacon (if using) in the bowl.
5. Top with nuts and dressing: Sprinkle the chopped walnuts or pecans over the salad. Drizzle with a low-sugar olive oil vinaigrette dressing to taste.

Nutritional Information: Calories: 400, Carbohydrates: 15g, Protein: 35g, Fat: 20g, Fiber: 5g

Tips:
- For a vegetarian option, omit the chicken and bacon and add additional protein sources like chickpeas or lentils.
- Use a low-carb tortilla on the side for a more filling meal.
- Experiment with different vegetables and toppings to customize the salad to your liking.
- Make sure to check the sugar content of any store-bought dressing and adjust the amount used accordingly.
- You can prepare the chicken and eggs in advance to save time on assembly.

Mediterranean Chickpea Salad

Prep Time: 10 minutes | **Cooking Time**: 10 minutes | **Total Time**: 20 minutes | **Serving Size**: 2-3

Ingredients:
- 1 can (15 oz.) chickpeas, drained and rinsed
- 1 cucumber, diced
- 1 red bell pepper, diced
- 1/2 cup cherry tomatoes, halved
- 1/4 cup red onion, finely diced (optional, use less for stronger flavor)
- 1/4 cup crumbled feta cheese (optional, use less for lower sodium)
- 1/4 cup chopped fresh parsley
- 1/4 cup chopped fresh mint (optional)
- 2 tablespoons extra virgin olive oil
- 1 tablespoon lemon juice
- 1/2 teaspoon dried oregano
- 1/4 teaspoon garlic powder
- Salt and freshly ground black pepper to taste

Optional Add-ins:
- 1/4 cup kalamata olives, pitted and halved
- 1/4 cup diced artichoke hearts
- 1 avocado, diced

Directions:
1. Roast chickpeas (optional): Preheat oven to 400°F (200°C). Toss chickpeas with 1 tablespoon olive oil and a pinch of salt. Spread on a baking sheet and roast for 10-15 minutes, until crispy.
2. Prepare vegetables: Dice cucumber, bell pepper, and red onion (if using). Halve cherry tomatoes. Roughly chop parsley and mint (if using).
3. Make dressing: In a small bowl, whisk together olive oil, lemon juice, oregano, garlic powder, salt, and pepper.
4. Assemble salad: Combine chickpeas, vegetables, herbs, and feta cheese (if using) in a large bowl.
5. Toss with dressing: Pour dressing over the salad and toss gently to coat all ingredients.
6. Serve immediately or chill for at least 30 minutes for flavors to meld.

Nutritional Information: Calories: 300, Carbohydrates: 30g, Fiber: 8g, Protein: 15g Fat: 10g, Sodium: 250mg

Tips:
- Use low-sodium feta cheese or omit it altogether to reduce sodium content.
- For a creamier texture, mash some of the chickpeas with a fork before adding them to the salad.
- Serve the salad on a bed of lettuce or spinach for added greens.
- Add crumbled whole-wheat pita bread or crackers for a satisfying crunch.
- Feel free to adjust the amount of dressing used based on your preference.

Taco Salad

Prep Time: 15 minutes | **Cooking Time**: 20 minutes | **Total Time**: 35 minutes | **Servings**: 2

Ingredients:
Protein:
- 1 pound lean ground chicken or turkey, browned (or 2 cups shredded cooked chicken)
- OR 1 can (15 oz.) black beans, drained and rinsed

Vegetables:
- 2 cups romaine lettuce, chopped
- 1 bell pepper, diced
- 1/2 cup cherry tomatoes, halved
- 1/4 cup red onion, diced
- 1 avocado, diced
- 1/4 cup fresh cilantro, chopped

Toppings:
- 1/2 cup low-fat cheddar cheese, shredded
- 1/4 cup salsa (choose a low-sugar option)
- 2 tablespoons plain Greek yogurt
- 1 tablespoon lime juice
- 1 teaspoon chili powder
- Salt and pepper to taste

Optional:
- 1/4 cup whole-wheat tortilla chips, crumbled
- 1/4 cup black olives, sliced

Directions:
1. Cook the protein: If using ground meat, brown it in a skillet over medium heat. Drain any excess fat. If using black beans, simply rinse and drain them.
2. Prepare the vegetables: Chop the lettuce, bell pepper, tomatoes, red onion, avocado, and cilantro.
3. Assemble the salad: Divide the lettuce between two bowls. Top with the cooked protein, vegetables, and cheese.
4. Make the dressing: In a small bowl, whisk together the yogurt, lime juice, chili powder, salt, and pepper.
5. Serve: Drizzle the dressing over the salad and top with salsa, cilantro, and optional toppings like tortilla chips and olives.

Nutritional Information: Calories: 450, Carbohydrates: 25g, Fiber: 8g, Protein: 30g, Fat: 20g

Tips:
- For a vegetarian option, omit the meat and use black beans as the protein source.
- You can use any type of lettuce you like.
- Feel free to add other vegetables, such as cucumber, corn, or jicama.
- Use a low-fat or fat-free cheese to reduce the fat content.
- Control your portion size, especially of the tortilla chips and salsa.
- Make sure to check the labels of all ingredients for hidden sugars and carbohydrates.

FISH AND SEAFOOD

Grilled Salmon with Lemon and Dill

Prep Time: 10 minutes | **Cooking Time**: 15 minutes | **Total Time**: 25 minutes | **Serving Size**: 2

Ingredients:
- 2 (6-ounce) skinless salmon fillets
- 1 tablespoon olive oil
- 1/2 teaspoon dried dill
- 1/4 teaspoon garlic powder
- 1/4 teaspoon black pepper
- 1/4 teaspoon salt (optional)
- 1 lemon, sliced
- Fresh dill sprigs, for garnish (optional)

Directions:
1. Preheat your grill to medium-high heat. If using a charcoal grill, let the coals ash over first.
2. In a small bowl, combine olive oil, dill, garlic powder, black pepper, and salt (if using).
3. Brush the salmon fillets with the olive oil mixture, coating both sides.
4. Place the salmon fillets on the preheated grill. Grill for 4-5 minutes per side, or until cooked through and opaque. The internal temperature should reach 145°F.
5. Remove the salmon from the grill and top with lemon slices. Garnish with fresh dill sprigs, if desired.

Nutritional Information: Calories: 350, Fat: 18g, Saturated Fat: 4g, Carbohydrates: 4g, Sugar: 1g, Protein: 35g, Sodium: 180mg

Tips:
- To prevent the salmon from sticking to the grill grates, lightly grease them with oil before placing the fish on.
- You can also bake the salmon in the oven at 400°F for 12-15 minutes, or until cooked through.
- For a more flavorful dish, marinate the salmon in the olive oil mixture for 30 minutes before grilling.
- Serve the grilled salmon with roasted vegetables, quinoa, or a side salad for a complete meal.

Shrimp Scampi

Prep Time: 10 minutes | **Cooking Time**: 15 minutes | **Total Time**: 25 minutes | **Servings**: 2

Ingredients:
- 1 tablespoon olive oil
- 2 cloves garlic, minced
- 1/4 cup dry white wine or vegetable broth
- 1/4 cup lemon juice
- 1/2 teaspoon dried oregano
- 1/4 teaspoon red pepper flakes (optional)
- 1/4 teaspoon black pepper
- 10 ounces assorted fish and seafood, such as:
- Sea scallops, cut into bite-sized pieces
- Cod or halibut, flaked
- Salmon, flaked
- Whitefish, flaked
- Mussels, steamed and debearded
- Squid rings, thawed
- 1 tablespoon chopped fresh parsley
- 1/4 cup cherry tomatoes, halved (optional)
- Cooked zucchini noodles or spaghetti squash (optional)

Directions:
1. Prepare the seafood: Choose your desired fish and seafood options. Thaw if frozen, clean and devein if necessary, and cut into bite-sized pieces. If using mussels, steam them beforehand and remove the meat from the shells.
2. Heat olive oil in a large skillet over medium heat. Add garlic and cook for 30 seconds, until fragrant. Be careful not to burn the garlic.
3. Deglaze the pan with white wine or broth. Add lemon juice, oregano, red pepper flakes (if using), and black pepper. Bring to a simmer and cook for 2 minutes.
4. Add the seafood. Gently stir to combine and cook for 3-5 minutes, depending on the chosen fish and seafood, until just cooked through. Do not overcook.
5. Stir in parsley and cherry tomatoes (if using). Heat through for another minute.
6. Serve immediately over cooked zucchini noodles or spaghetti squash (optional).

Tips:
- Adjust the amount of red pepper flakes based on your desired spice level.
- For a richer flavor, add 1 tablespoon of butter with the olive oil.
- Serve with a side of steamed broccoli or roasted Brussels sprouts for a complete meal.
- To further reduce carbohydrates, skip the optional pasta substitute.
- If using shrimp, adjust the cooking time according to size. Larger shrimp will cook in 2-3 minutes, while smaller shrimp might only need 1-2 minutes.
- Make sure to choose low-mercury fish options when selecting your seafood.

Baked Cod with Herbs

Prep Time: 10 minutes | **Cooking Time**: 15-20 minutes | **Total Time**: 25-30 minutes | **Serving Size**: 4 servings

Ingredients:

- 4 (4-ounce) cod fillets
- 1 tablespoon olive oil
- 1/2 teaspoon dried oregano
- 1/2 teaspoon dried thyme
- 1/4 teaspoon garlic powder
- 1/4 teaspoon paprika
- Salt and pepper to taste
- 1 lemon, sliced (optional)
- Fresh herbs (parsley, dill, etc.) for garnish (optional)

Directions:

1. Preheat oven to 400°F (200°C). Line a baking sheet with parchment paper.
2. In a small bowl, combine olive oil, oregano, thyme, garlic powder, paprika, salt, and pepper.
3. Brush the cod fillets with the herb mixture, coating them evenly.
4. Place the cod fillets on the prepared baking sheet.
5. Bake for 15-20 minutes, or until the cod is cooked through and flakes easily with a fork.
6. (Optional) Garnish with lemon slices and fresh herbs before serving.

Nutritional Information: Calories: 220, Carbohydrates: 5g, Fiber: 1g, Net Carbs: 4g, Protein: 30g, Fat: 7g, Saturated Fat: 1g

Tips:

- You can substitute any other white fish for the cod, such as haddock, tilapia, or halibut.
- For a more vibrant flavor, add a squeeze of fresh lemon juice to the herb mixture.
- Serve the cod with roasted vegetables, quinoa, or brown rice for a complete meal.
- To make this recipe ahead of time, bake the cod as directed and then store it in the refrigerator for up to 3 days. Reheat in the oven or microwave before serving.

Cajun Spiced Tilapia

Prep Time: 5 minutes | **Cooking Time**: 10-12 minutes | **Total Time**: 15-17 minutes | **Serving Size**: 1

Ingredients:

- 1 (4-6 oz.) tilapia fillet
- 1 tbsp. olive oil
- 1 tsp. Cajun seasoning (choose a low-sodium option if needed)
- 1/4 tsp. black pepper
- 1/4 cup chopped green onion (optional)
- 1/4 cup chopped bell pepper (optional)
- 1/4 cup cherry tomatoes (optional)
- Lemon wedge (optional)

Directions:

1. Preheat: Heat olive oil in a non-stick skillet over medium heat.
2. Season Tilapia: Pat the tilapia dry and season with Cajun seasoning and black pepper.
3. Cook Tilapia: Place the tilapia in the hot skillet and cook for 4-5 minutes per side, or until cooked through and flakes easily with a fork.
4. Optional Vegetables: If using, add green onion, bell pepper, and cherry tomatoes to the skillet around the tilapia during the last 2-3 minutes of cooking.
5. Serve: Plate the tilapia with desired vegetables and squeeze a lemon wedge over it for added flavor (optional).

Nutritional Information: Calories: 220, Carbohydrates: 2g, Fiber: 0g, Sugars: 0g, Protein: 32g, Fat: 8g, Saturated Fat: 2g, Cholesterol: 70mg, Sodium: 350mg

Tips:

- Use a low-sodium Cajun seasoning to keep the sodium content in check.
- Adjust the amount of Cajun seasoning to your spice preference.
- Serve with a side of roasted vegetables, brown rice, or quinoa for a complete meal.
- You can substitute other lean fish or seafood for the tilapia, such as cod, shrimp, or scallops.
- For a thicker Cajun sauce, mix 1 tablespoon of cornstarch with 2 tablespoons of water and stir into the pan after removing the fish. Cook for another minute until thickened.

Lemon Garlic Butter Shrimp

Prep Time: 10 minutes | **Cooking Time**: 15 minutes | **Total Time**: 25 minutes | **Servings**: 2

Ingredients:
- 1 pound large shrimp, peeled and deveined
- 1 tablespoon olive oil
- 2 tablespoons unsalted butter
- 3 cloves garlic, minced
- 1/4 teaspoon dried oregano
- Pinch of red pepper flakes (optional)
- 1/4 cup dry white wine or low-sodium chicken broth
- 1/4 cup fresh lemon juice
- 1 tablespoon chopped fresh parsley
- Salt and freshly ground black pepper, to taste

Directions:
1. Prep: Pat the shrimp dry with paper towels. In a small bowl, combine the oregano, red pepper flakes (if using), and salt and pepper. Season the shrimp with the spice mixture.
2. Cook: Heat the olive oil in a large skillet over medium heat. Add the shrimp and cook, stirring occasionally, until pink and opaque, about 3-4 minutes per side. Remove the shrimp from the pan and set aside.
3. Garlic Butter Sauce: Add the butter to the pan and melt over medium heat. Add the garlic and cook until fragrant, about 30 seconds. Pour in the white wine or broth and scrape up any browned bits from the bottom of the pan. Let the sauce simmer for 1 minute.
4. Finish: Stir in the lemon juice and parsley. Bring the sauce to a simmer and return the shrimp to the pan. Cook for 1-2 minutes more, until the shrimp is heated through and the sauce is slightly thickened.
5. Serve: Serve immediately over a bed of steamed vegetables, cauliflower rice, or quinoa.

Nutritional Information: Calories: 300, Carbohydrates: 5g, Fat: 15g, Protein: 25g Sodium: 300mg

Tips:
- For a richer flavor, use a combination of butter and olive oil.
- You can adjust the amount of garlic to your preference.
- If you don't have white wine or broth, you can substitute water.
- Add a squeeze of fresh lemon juice before serving for an extra burst of flavor.
- Make sure not to overcook the shrimp, as it will become tough and rubbery.
- For a low-carb option, serve with roasted vegetables instead of rice or pasta.

Tuna Steak Salad

Prep Time: 10 minutes | **Cooking Time**: 5 minutes | **Total Time**: 15 minutes | **Serving Size**: 1

Ingredients:
- 1 (6-ounce) tuna steak
- 2 tablespoons olive oil, divided
- Salt and freshly ground black pepper, to taste
- 2 cups mixed greens
- 1/2 cup cherry tomatoes, halved
- 1/4 cup cucumber, diced
- 1/4 red onion, thinly sliced
- 1/4 cup crumbled feta cheese (optional)
- Lemon Vinaigrette:
- 2 tablespoons olive oil
- 1 tablespoon lemon juice
- 1/2 teaspoon Dijon mustard
- 1/4 teaspoon dried oregano
- Pinch of salt and pepper

Directions:
1. Prepare the vinaigrette: In a small bowl, whisk together olive oil, lemon juice, Dijon mustard, oregano, salt, and pepper. Set aside.
2. Season and cook the tuna: Pat the tuna steak dry with paper towels. Season generously with salt and pepper. Heat 1 tablespoon olive oil in a pan over medium-high heat. Sear the tuna for 2-3 minutes per side, or until cooked to desired doneness (medium-rare is recommended). Let the tuna rest for 5 minutes before slicing.
3. Assemble the salad: In a large bowl, combine mixed greens, tomatoes, cucumber, red onion, and feta cheese (if using).
4. Slice the tuna: Using a sharp knife, slice the tuna steak into thin strips.
5. Dress and serve: Add the sliced tuna to the salad bowl. Drizzle with the lemon vinaigrette and toss gently to combine. Serve immediately.

Nutritional Information: Calories: 350, Fat: 12g, Carbohydrates: 10g (4g fiber), Protein: 35g, Sodium: 300mg

Tips:
- Use a low-sodium soy sauce to further reduce the sodium content.
- Add other vegetables to the salad, such as bell peppers, olives, or artichoke hearts.
- Substitute the feta cheese with crumbled goat cheese or ricotta cheese for a lower-fat option.
- For a heartier salad, serve on a bed of quinoa or brown rice.
- You can also grill the tuna steak instead of pan-searing it.
- Be sure to check the mercury content of the tuna you buy. Choose varieties with lower mercury levels, such as albacore or skipjack.

Garlic Herb Grilled Swordfish

Prep Time: 10 minutes | **Cooking Time**: 7-10 minutes | **Total Time**: 17-20 minutes | **Servings**: 2

Ingredients:
- 2 swordfish steaks (6-8oz each), skinless
- 2 tablespoons olive oil
- 1 tablespoon lemon juice
- 1/2 teaspoon dried oregano
- 1/4 teaspoon dried thyme
- 1/4 teaspoon garlic powder
- 1/4 teaspoon onion powder
- Pinch of black pepper
- Fresh herbs (optional): parsley, chives, dill

Directions:
1. Preheat your grill to medium-high heat. If using a charcoal grill, wait for the coals to be white-hot.
2. Prepare the marinade: In a small bowl, whisk together olive oil, lemon juice, oregano, thyme, garlic powder, onion powder, and black pepper.
3. Marinate the swordfish: Place the swordfish steaks in a shallow dish and pour the marinade over them. Coat both sides of the fish and let marinate for 10 minutes, or longer if time allows.
4. Grill the swordfish: When the grill is hot, lightly oil the grates. Remove the swordfish from the marinade and discard any excess. Place the fish on the grill and cook for 3-4 minutes per side, or until cooked through and opaque.
5. Optional: If desired, brush the fish with additional marinade during the last minute of cooking.
6. Serve immediately. Garnish with fresh herbs, if using.

Nutritional Information: Calories: 220, Fat: 7g, Saturated Fat: 1g, Carbohydrates: 0g, Sugar: 0g, Protein: 35g, Sodium: 300mg

Tips:
- To check for doneness, insert a fork into the thickest part of the fish. It should flake easily when gently pressed.
- If you don't have fresh herbs, you can use 1/2 teaspoon of each dried herb instead.
- Serve with a side of grilled vegetables or a diabetic-friendly salad for a complete meal.
- For a more flavorful crust, sprinkle the fish with a pinch of sea salt before grilling.
- Leftovers can be stored in the refrigerator for up to 2 days.

Coconut Curry Shrimp

Prep Time: 15 minutes **Cooking Time**: 20 minutes | **Total Time**: 35 minutes **Servings**: 4

Ingredients:
- 1 tablespoon olive oil
- 1 medium onion, diced
- 2 cloves garlic, minced
- 1 tablespoon grated ginger
- 1 teaspoon ground turmeric
- 1/2 teaspoon ground cumin
- 1/4 teaspoon chili powder (optional, for a touch of heat)
- 1 can (13.5 ounces) light coconut milk
- 1 cup low-sodium chicken broth
- 1/2 cup bell pepper, diced (red, yellow, or orange)
- 1/2 cup broccoli florets
- 1 cup cherry tomatoes, halved
- 1 pound large shrimp, peeled and deveined
- 1/4 cup chopped fresh cilantro
- 1 tablespoon lime juice
- Salt and black pepper to taste

Directions:
1. Heat oil in a large skillet or wok over medium heat. Add onion and cook until softened, about 5 minutes. Stir in garlic and ginger and cook for another minute, until fragrant.
2. Add turmeric, cumin, and chili powder (if using) and cook for 30 seconds. Stir in coconut milk and chicken broth, scraping up any browned bits from the bottom of the pan. Bring to a simmer.
3. Add bell pepper, broccoli, and tomatoes. Simmer for 5 minutes, or until vegetables are tender-crisp.
4. Add shrimp and cook for 5-7 minutes, or until pink and cooked through. Stir occasionally.
5. Remove from heat and stir in cilantro and lime juice. Season with salt and pepper to taste.
6. Serve immediately over a bed of cauliflower rice or brown rice.

Nutritional Information: Calories: 350, Carbohydrates: 25g, Fiber: 3g, Net Carbs: 22g, Protein: 30g, Fat: 15g, Saturated Fat: 8g, Cholesterol: 200mg, Sodium: 350mg

Tips:
- For a thicker sauce, mix 1 tablespoon cornstarch with 2 tablespoons water in a small bowl. Stir into the simmering sauce and cook until thickened.
- Feel free to add other low-carb vegetables like zucchini, green beans, or snow peas.
- Adjust the amount of chili powder according to your desired spice level.
- You can use frozen shrimp, but thaw them completely before adding them to the pan.
- For a richer flavor, use full-fat coconut milk, but be aware that it will increase the calorie and fat content.
- Be sure to check the nutrition labels of all ingredients you use, as sodium content can vary.

Baked Lemon Garlic Butter Scallops

Prep Time: 10 minutes | **Cooking Time**: 15 minutes | **Total Time**: 25 minutes | **Serving Size**: 2

Ingredients:

- 12 large sea scallops, side muscle removed and patted dry
- 1 tablespoon olive oil
- 2 tablespoons unsalted butter, melted
- 2 cloves garlic, minced
- 1/4 cup chopped fresh parsley
- 1 tablespoon lemon juice
- 1/4 teaspoon dried thyme
- 1/8 teaspoon black pepper
- Pinch of salt (optional)

Directions:

1. Preheat oven to 400°F (200°C). Line a baking sheet with parchment paper.
2. In a small bowl, whisk together olive oil, melted butter, garlic, parsley, lemon juice, thyme, and pepper.
3. Arrange scallops on the prepared baking sheet. Season with salt (optional) to taste.
4. Spoon the lemon garlic butter mixture evenly over the scallops.
5. Bake for 10-12 minutes, or until the scallops are opaque and cooked through.
6. Broil for the last 2-3 minutes for a golden brown crust (optional).
7. Serve immediately with your favorite low-carb side dish, such as roasted vegetables, cauliflower rice, or quinoa.

Nutritional Information: Calories: 300, Carbohydrates: 5g, Protein: 25g, Fat: 20g, Sodium: 200mg

Tips:

- For a richer flavor, use a combination of butter and olive oil.
- Add a pinch of red pepper flakes for a touch of heat.
- If you don't have fresh parsley, you can use 1/2 teaspoon dried parsley.
- Be sure to not overcook the scallops, as they will become tough.
- For a more decadent twist, drizzle the scallops with balsamic glaze before serving.

Miso Glazed Grilled Sea Bass

Prep Time: 15 minutes | **Cooking Time**: 15 minutes | **Total Time**: 30 minutes | **Serving Size**: 2

Ingredients:

- 2 skin-on sea bass fillets (6-8 oz. each)
- 2 tablespoons white miso paste
- 1 tablespoon sake
- 1 tablespoon mirin (optional, can use more white miso paste)
- 1 tablespoon low-sodium soy sauce
- 1 tablespoon rice vinegar
- 1 tablespoon honey (or other low-glycemic sweetener like erythritol)
- 1 tablespoon olive oil
- 1 teaspoon grated ginger
- 1/2 teaspoon garlic powder
- 1/4 teaspoon black pepper
- 1 scallion, sliced (optional, for garnish)

Directions:

1. Prepare the marinade: In a small bowl, whisk together miso paste, sake, mirin (if using), soy sauce, rice vinegar, honey, olive oil, ginger, garlic powder, and black pepper.
2. Marinate the fish: Place the sea bass fillets in a shallow dish and pour the marinade over them. Cover and refrigerate for at least 15 minutes, or up to 30 minutes for deeper flavor.
3. Preheat the grill: Preheat your grill to medium-high heat. If using a charcoal grill, let the coals ash over before cooking.
4. Grill the fish: Remove the fish from the marinade and discard the marinade. Place the fish fillets skin-side down on the preheated grill. Cook for 5-7 minutes, or until the skin is crispy and golden brown.
5. Flip and glaze: Carefully flip the fish and brush with any remaining marinade in the dish. Cook for an additional 3-5 minutes, or until the fish is cooked through and flakes easily with a fork.
6. Serve: Transfer the fish to serving plates and garnish with sliced scallions (optional).

Nutritional Information: Calories: 350, Carbohydrates: 15g, Sugars: 5g, Protein: 30g, Fat: 15g, Saturated fat: 2g, Sodium: 500mg

Tips:
- Choose low-sodium miso paste to reduce the sodium content.
- Adjust the amount of honey or other sweetener to your taste preference and dietary needs.
- Consider using brown rice, quinoa, or roasted vegetables as diabetic-friendly side dishes.
- Monitor your blood sugar levels before and after consuming this dish.

POULTRY

Grilled Lemon Herb Chicken

Prep Time: 10 minutes | **Cooking Time**: 25-30 minutes | **Total Time**: 35-40 minutes | **Serving Size**: 4

Ingredients:
- 4 boneless, skinless chicken breasts (about 6oz each)
- 1/4 cup olive oil
- 2 tablespoons lemon juice
- 2 tablespoons chopped fresh parsley
- 1 tablespoon chopped fresh thyme
- 1 teaspoon dried oregano
- 1/2 teaspoon garlic powder
- 1/4 teaspoon black pepper
- 1/4 teaspoon salt (optional, adjust to taste)
- 1 lemon, sliced (optional)

Directions:
1. Prepare the marinade: In a bowl, whisk together olive oil, lemon juice, parsley, thyme, oregano, garlic powder, pepper, and salt (if using).
2. Marinate the chicken: Place the chicken breasts in a single layer in a shallow dish or large zip-top bag. Pour the marinade over the chicken, coating it evenly. Cover or seal the bag and marinate in the refrigerator for at least 30 minutes, or up to 4 hours for deeper flavor.
3. Preheat the grill: Prepare your grill for medium-high heat. If using a charcoal grill, light the coals and let them burn until white hot. If using a gas grill, preheat to medium-high for 10-15 minutes.
4. Grill the chicken: Place the chicken breasts on the preheated grill, discarding any excess marinade. Grill for 5-7 minutes per side, or until the chicken is cooked through and reaches an internal temperature of 165°F.
5. Optional lemon slices: During the last few minutes of grilling, you can add lemon slices to the grill alongside the chicken for a smoky lemon flavor.
6. Rest and serve: Remove the chicken from the grill and let it rest for 5-10 minutes before serving. This allows the juices to redistribute, resulting in juicier chicken.
7. Serve: Enjoy the grilled chicken on its own, with grilled vegetables, or over a bed of salad greens. Garnish with additional fresh herbs and lemon wedges, if desired.

Nutritional Information: Calories: 350, Carbohydrates: 5g, Fat: 20g, 5g Saturated Fat: 5g, Protein: 40g, Sodium: 250mg

Tips:
- For an extra burst of flavor, marinate the chicken overnight.
- If you don't have fresh herbs, you can use 1 teaspoon each of dried parsley, thyme, and oregano.
- Be careful not to overcook the chicken, as it can become dry. Use a meat thermometer to check the internal temperature.
- If you are watching your sodium intake, omit the salt or use a low-sodium marinade.
- Serve with diabetic-friendly sides like roasted vegetables, whole-wheat bread, or a green salad with a light vinaigrette dressing.

Baked Garlic Parmesan Turkey Meatballs

Prep Time: 15 minutes | **Cooking Time**: 20 minutes | **Total Time**: 35 minutes | **Serving Size**: 4 servings

Ingredients:

- 1 pound ground turkey (93% lean)
- 1/2 cup grated Parmesan cheese
- 1/4 cup chopped fresh parsley
- 1/4 cup chopped fresh basil
- 1/4 cup chopped onion
- 2 cloves garlic, minced
- 1 egg, beaten
- 1/4 cup panko breadcrumbs
- 1 teaspoon dried oregano
- 1/2 teaspoon salt
- 1/4 teaspoon black pepper
- 1/4 cup marinara sauce, sugar-free (optional)

Directions:

1. Preheat oven to 400°F (200°C). Line a baking sheet with parchment paper.
2. In a large bowl, combine ground turkey, Parmesan cheese, parsley, basil, onion, garlic, egg, breadcrumbs, oregano, salt, and pepper. Mix well until combined.
3. Roll the mixture into 1-inch meatballs. Place on the prepared baking sheet.
4. (Optional) Drizzle meatballs with marinara sauce.
5. Bake for 20 minutes, or until internal temperature reaches 165°F (74°C).
6. Serve immediately with additional marinara sauce, if desired.

Nutritional Information: Calories: 300, Fat: 8g, Carbohydrates: 10g, Fiber: 2g, Protein: 30g, Sodium: 300mg

Tips:

- For a moister meatball, add 1/4 cup grated zucchini or finely chopped mushrooms to the mixture.
- Use a cookie scoop for uniform sized meatballs.
- Freeze any leftover meatballs for future meals.
- Serve with low-carb sides like roasted vegetables, zucchini noodles, or cauliflower rice.
- Adjust the amount of marinara sauce and cheese based on your individual carbohydrate needs.

Rosemary Roasted Chicken Thighs

Prep Time: 10 minutes | **Cooking Time**: 40 minutes | **Total Time**: 50 minutes | **Serving Size**: 4

Ingredients:

- 4 bone-in, skin-on chicken thighs (about 1.5 lbs.)
- 1 tablespoon olive oil
- 1 tablespoon chopped fresh rosemary
- 1/2 teaspoon garlic powder
- 1/4 teaspoon onion powder
- 1/4 teaspoon black pepper
- 1/4 teaspoon paprika (optional)
- Pinch of salt (optional)
- 1/2 cup low-sodium chicken broth
- 1 tablespoon lemon juice (optional)

Directions:

1. Preheat oven to 425°F (220°C). Line a baking sheet with parchment paper.
2. Pat the chicken thighs dry with paper towels.
3. In a small bowl, combine olive oil, rosemary, garlic powder, onion powder, pepper, and paprika (if using). Rub the mixture onto the chicken thighs, coating them evenly.
4. Arrange the chicken thighs on the prepared baking sheet, skin-side up.
5. In a separate bowl, mix together chicken broth and lemon juice (if using). Pour the mixture around the chicken thighs in the baking sheet.
6. Bake for 25 minutes.
7. Reduce oven temperature to 375°F (190°C) and bake for an additional 15 minutes, or until the chicken is cooked through and the internal temperature reaches 165°F (74°C). The juices should run clear when pierced with a fork.
8. Let the chicken rest for 5 minutes before serving.

Nutritional Information: Calories: 350, Carbohydrates: 5g, Fat: 30g, Protein: 35g, Sodium: 300mg

Tips:

- For extra crispy skin, pat the chicken thighs very dry before seasoning and roasting.
- You can add other vegetables to the baking sheet, such as chopped carrots, onions, or potatoes, for a complete meal.
- If you are monitoring your sodium intake, be mindful of the amount of salt you add. You can taste the chicken after roasting and adjust the seasoning as needed.
- Serve with a low-carbohydrate side dish, such as roasted vegetables, steamed broccoli, or a side salad.

Lemon Garlic Herb Turkey Breast

Prep Time: 15 minutes | **Cooking Time**: 1 hour 20 minutes | **Total Time**: 1 hour 35 minutes | **Servings**: 4

Ingredients:
- 1 boneless, skinless turkey breast (about 1.5kg/3.3 lbs)
- 2 tablespoons olive oil
- 4 cloves garlic, minced
- 1 tablespoon chopped fresh rosemary
- 1 tablespoon chopped fresh thyme
- 1/2 teaspoon dried oregano
- 1/4 teaspoon black pepper
- 1/4 teaspoon salt (optional, use to taste)
- 1 lemon, zested and juiced
- 1/2 cup chicken broth (low-sodium)

Directions:
1. Preheat oven to 375°F (190°C).
2. Pat the turkey breast dry with paper towels.
3. In a small bowl, whisk together olive oil, garlic, rosemary, thyme, oregano, pepper, and salt (if using).
4. Rub the herb mixture all over the turkey breast, getting under the skin as much as possible.
5. Place the turkey breast in a roasting pan. Scatter lemon zest around the turkey.
6. In a separate bowl, stir together lemon juice and chicken broth.
7. Pour the broth mixture around the turkey in the roasting pan.
8. Cover the roasting pan with foil and bake for 45 minutes.
9. Remove the foil and continue baking for another 35-45 minutes, or until the internal temperature of the turkey reaches 165°F (74°C) when measured with a meat thermometer.
10. Let the turkey rest for 10 minutes before slicing and serving.

Nutritional Information: Calories: 350, Carbohydrates: 5g, Fat: 20g, Saturated Fat: 5g, Protein: 40g, Sodium: 300mg

Tips:
- For extra flavor, add a few thin lemon slices to the roasting pan along with the zest.
- If you prefer a crispier skin, remove the foil for the last 15 minutes of baking.
- Serve with low-carbohydrate sides like roasted vegetables, green salad, or cauliflower rice.
- To further reduce carbohydrates, use unsweetened lemon juice and herbs.
- You can adjust the amount of herbs and spices to your taste.

Cilantro Lime Grilled Chicken

Prep Time: 15 minutes | **Cooking Time**: 20-25 minutes | **Total Time**: 35-40 minutes | **Serving Size**: 4 servings

Ingredients:
- 1 pound boneless, skinless chicken breasts or thighs
- 2 tablespoons olive oil
- 2 tablespoons freshly squeezed lime juice
- 1 tablespoon chopped fresh cilantro
- 1/2 teaspoon ground cumin
- 1/4 teaspoon garlic powder
- 1/4 teaspoon chili powder (optional)
- Salt and black pepper to taste
- Lime wedges and additional cilantro for garnish (optional)

Directions:
1. Prepare the marinade: In a bowl, whisk together the olive oil, lime juice, cilantro, cumin, garlic powder, chili powder (if using), salt, and pepper.
2. Marinate the chicken: Place the chicken in a shallow dish and pour the marinade over it. Cover and refrigerate for at least 30 minutes, or up to 2 hours for deeper flavor.
3. Preheat the grill: Preheat your grill to medium-high heat. If using a charcoal grill, ensure the coals are white-hot.
4. Grill the chicken: Remove the chicken from the marinade and discard any remaining marinade. Grill the chicken for 5-7 minutes per side, or until cooked through and juices run clear. An instant-read thermometer inserted into the thickest part of the chicken should reach 165°F (74°C).
5. Serve: Let the chicken rest for a few minutes before slicing and serving. Garnish with lime wedges and additional cilantro, if desired.

Nutritional Information: Calories: 250, Carbohydrates: 4g, Fat: 12g, Protein: 35g, Sodium: 200mg

Tips:
- For a smoky flavor, you can add a teaspoon of smoked paprika to the marinade.
- If you don't have fresh cilantro, you can substitute 1/2 teaspoon of dried cilantro.
- To add some sweetness without added sugar, use a squeeze of stevia or a sugar substitute approved for diabetics.
- Serve the chicken with grilled vegetables, a side salad, or brown rice for a complete meal.
- Adjust the amount of chili powder according to your desired spice level.

Pesto Baked Chicken

Prep Time: 10 minutes | **Cooking Time**: 25 minutes | **Total Time**: 35 minutes | **Serving Size**: 4

Ingredients:

- 4 boneless, skinless chicken breasts (thinly sliced)
- 1/2 cup reduced-sodium pesto
- 1/4 cup cherry tomatoes, halved
- 1/4 cup crumbled feta cheese
- 1 tablespoon olive oil
- 1/2 teaspoon dried oregano
- 1/4 teaspoon garlic powder
- Salt and pepper to taste

Directions:

1. Preheat oven to 400°F (200°C). Line a baking sheet with parchment paper.
2. In a bowl, combine olive oil, oregano, garlic powder, salt, and pepper.
3. Toss chicken breasts in the olive oil mixture until evenly coated.
4. Spread pesto evenly over the bottom of the prepared baking sheet.
5. Arrange chicken breasts on top of the pesto.
6. Top with cherry tomatoes and feta cheese.
7. Bake for 20-25 minutes, or until chicken is cooked through and internal temperature reaches 165°F (74°C).
8. Broil for the last 2-3 minutes to brown the cheese, if desired.

Nutritional Information: Calories: 350, Carbohydrates: 10g, Protein: 40g, Fat: 15g, Sodium: 300mg

Tips:

- Use a low-carb pesto to further reduce the carbohydrate content of the dish.
- Add other vegetables to the recipe, such as roasted peppers, zucchini, or broccoli.
- Serve with a side of low-carb roasted vegetables or a salad.
- You can also use boneless, skinless chicken thighs in this recipe. Just be sure to adjust the cooking time, as thighs take longer to cook through than breasts.

Sesame Ginger Chicken Stir-Fry

Prep Time: 15 minutes | **Cooking Time**: 15 minutes | **Total Time**: 30 minutes | **Serving Size**: 2 servings

Ingredients:

For the marinade:
- 1 tbsp. low-sodium soy sauce
- 1 tbsp. rice vinegar
- 1 tsp. toasted sesame oil
- 1/2 tsp. grated ginger
- 1 clove garlic, minced
- 1/4 tsp. black pepper

For the stir-fry:
- 1 pound boneless, skinless chicken breasts, thinly sliced
- 1 tbsp. canola oil
- 1 cup broccoli florets
- 1 cup bell pepper (any color), sliced
- 1/2 cup snow peas
- 1/4 cup sliced green onions
- 1 tbsp. cornstarch
- 1/4 cup chicken broth
- 1 tbsp. low-sodium soy sauce
- 1 tsp. rice vinegar
- 1/2 tsp. sesame oil
- 1/4 tsp. sriracha (optional)
- Sesame seeds, for garnish

Directions:
1. Marinate the chicken: In a bowl, whisk together the soy sauce, rice vinegar, sesame oil, ginger, garlic, and black pepper. Add the chicken and toss to coat. Marinate for at least 15 minutes, or up to 30 minutes.
2. Prepare the vegetables: Wash and chop the broccoli, bell pepper, snow peas, and green onions.
3. Cook the chicken: Heat the canola oil in a large skillet or wok over medium-high heat. Add the chicken and cook for 5-7 minutes, or until cooked through. Remove from the pan and set aside.
4. Stir-fry the vegetables: Add the broccoli, bell pepper, and snow peas to the pan. Cook for 3-4 minutes, or until crisp-tender.
5. Make the sauce: In a small bowl, whisk together the cornstarch, chicken broth, soy sauce, rice vinegar, sesame oil, and sriracha (if using).
6. Combine and serve: Add the chicken back to the pan with the vegetables. Pour in the sauce and cook for 1-2 minutes, or until the sauce thickens and coats the ingredients.
7. Garnish and serve: Sprinkle with sesame seeds and serve immediately with brown rice or quinoa.

Nutritional Information: Calories: 400, Carbohydrates: 20g, Protein: 30g, Fat: 15g, Sodium: 500mg

Tips:
- Use a low-sodium soy sauce to keep the sodium content in check.
- Adjust the amount of sriracha to your desired level of spiciness.
- Serve with a side of steamed edamame for additional protein and fiber.
- You can add other vegetables to this stir-fry, such as carrots, snap peas, or zucchini.
- If you don't have sriracha, you can use another chili sauce or paste.
- Leftovers can be stored in an airtight container in the refrigerator for up to 3 days.

Honey Mustard Glazed Chicken

Prep Time: 10 minutes | **Cooking Time**: 30 minutes | **Total Time**: 40 minutes | **Serving** Size: 4 servings

Ingredients:
- 4 boneless, skinless chicken breasts (thinned to even thickness)
- 1 tablespoon olive oil
- 1/4 teaspoon dried thyme
- 1/4 teaspoon garlic powder
- 1/4 teaspoon black pepper
- 1/4 cup Dijon mustard (reduced-sodium)
- 1/4 cup honey (substitute with sugar-free maple syrup or erythritol for lower sugar)
- 1 tablespoon apple cider vinegar
- 1/4 cup water
- 1 tablespoon chopped fresh parsley (optional, for garnish)

Directions:
1. Preheat oven to 400°F (200°C). Line a baking sheet with parchment paper.
2. In a small bowl, combine olive oil, thyme, garlic powder, and black pepper. Rub the mixture onto both sides of the chicken breasts.
3. In another bowl, whisk together Dijon mustard, honey, apple cider vinegar, and water until smooth.
4. Place chicken breasts on the prepared baking sheet. Brush half of the glaze over the chicken.
5. Bake for 20 minutes. Flip the chicken breasts and brush with the remaining glaze.
6. Bake for an additional 10-15 minutes, or until the chicken is cooked through and reaches an internal temperature of 165°F (74°C).
7. Garnish with chopped parsley (optional) and serve immediately.

Nutritional Information: Calories: 350, Carbohydrates: 25g, Sugar: 10g, Protein: 30g, Fat: 15g, Saturated Fat: 4g, Cholesterol: 70mg, Sodium: 400mg

Tips:
- Use a meat thermometer to ensure the chicken is cooked through.
- For a thicker glaze, simmer the glaze in a saucepan over low heat for a few minutes before using.
- Serve with roasted vegetables, brown rice, or quinoa for a complete and balanced meal.
- You can substitute Dijon mustard with other mustards like whole-grain or spicy brown mustard, but adjust the sweetness of the glaze accordingly.
- For a crispy crust, broil the chicken for the last few minutes of cooking, watching closely to avoid burning.

Herb-Roasted Quail

Prep Time: 15 minutes | **Cooking Time**: 25-30 minutes | **Total Time**: 40-45 minutes | **Serving Size**: 1

Ingredients:
- 2 quail, cleaned and patted dry
- 1 tablespoon olive oil
- 1/2 teaspoon dried thyme
- 1/2 teaspoon dried rosemary
- 1/4 teaspoon dried sage
- Pinch of salt and black pepper
- 1/2 lemon, sliced
- 2 cloves garlic, smashed
- 1/4 cup chopped fresh herbs (such as parsley, chives, dill)
- Optional: 1/2 cup sugar-free broth or water

Directions:
1. Preheat oven to 400°F (200°C).
2. In a small bowl, combine olive oil, thyme, rosemary, sage, salt, and pepper. Rub the mixture evenly over the quail.
3. Place the quail in a baking dish, breast-side up. Arrange lemon slices and garlic cloves around the quail.
4. Pour in the optional broth or water (this helps prevent the quail from drying out).
5. Cover the baking dish with foil and bake for 20 minutes.
6. Remove the foil and bake for an additional 10-15 minutes, or until the quail are cooked through and golden brown. The internal temperature should reach 165°F (74°C).
7. Let the quail rest for 5 minutes before serving.
8. Garnish with fresh herbs and enjoy

Nutritional Information: Calories: 250, Protein: 30g, Fat: 10g, Carbohydrates: 5g, Sugar: 2g, Sodium: 150mg

Tips:
- You can adjust the herbs and spices to your liking. Other options include oregano, basil, or tarragon.
- If you are using frozen quail, be sure to thaw them completely before roasting.
- For a richer flavor, you can stuff the quail cavity with chopped vegetables, such as onions, carrots, or celery.
- Serve the quail with roasted vegetables, a low-carb salad, or quinoa.
- Be sure to monitor your blood sugar levels before and after consuming this dish.

Greek Yogurt Marinated Chicken Skewers

Prep Time: 15 minutes | **Cooking Time**: 15-20 minutes | **Total Time**: 30-35 minutes | **Servings**: 4

Ingredients:
- 1 pound boneless, skinless chicken thighs, cut into 1-inch cubes
- 1 cup plain Greek yogurt
- 2 tablespoons olive oil
- 2 tablespoons lemon juice
- 1 tablespoon chopped fresh rosemary
- 1 teaspoon dried oregano
- 1/2 teaspoon garlic powder
- 30 minutes
- 1/4 teaspoon black pepper
- 1/4 teaspoon ground cinnamon (optional)
- 1 medium red onion, cut into wedges
- 1 bell pepper, cut into chunks
- 1 zucchini, cut into chunks
- Wooden skewers, soaked in water for at least

Directions:
1. In a large bowl, whisk together Greek yogurt, olive oil, lemon juice, rosemary, oregano, garlic powder, black pepper, and cinnamon (if using).
2. Add chicken cubes to the marinade and toss to coat evenly. Cover and refrigerate for at least 30 minutes, or up to 4 hours.
3. Preheat grill or grill pan to medium-high heat.
4. Thread chicken pieces and vegetables onto soaked skewers, alternating colors and textures for visual appeal.
5. Grill skewers for 10-15 minutes per side, or until chicken is cooked through and vegetables are tender-crisp.
6. Serve immediately with desired sides, such as a side salad, roasted vegetables, or whole-wheat pita bread.

Nutritional Information: Calories: 300, Carbohydrates: 15g, Protein: 35g, Fat: 10g
Sodium: 350mg

Tips:
- For a thicker marinade, use full-fat Greek yogurt.
- Substitute chicken breasts for thighs if preferred, but be aware that they may dry out more easily.
- Add other vegetables to the skewers, such as cherry tomatoes, mushrooms, or eggplant.
- If you don't have fresh herbs, use 1/2 teaspoon dried rosemary and 1/4 teaspoon dried oregano.
- For a smoky flavor, add 1/4 teaspoon smoked paprika to the marinade.
- Serve with a low-sugar dipping sauce, such as tzatziki sauce or a vinaigrette made with olive oil and lemon juice.

BEEF AND PORK

Grilled Sirloin Steak with Herb Marinade

Prep Time: 15 minutes | **Cooking Time**: 15-20 minutes | **Total Time**: 30-35 minutes | **Servings**: 4

Ingredients:
- 1 pound boneless, skinless chicken breasts or thighs, cut into 1-inch cubes
- 1 cup plain Greek yogurt (2% or non-fat)
- 2 tablespoons olive oil
- 2 tablespoons lemon juice
- 1 tablespoon chopped fresh oregano or 1 teaspoon dried oregano
- 1 teaspoon garlic powder
- 1/2 teaspoon paprika
- 1/4 teaspoon salt
- 1/4 teaspoon black pepper
- Wooden skewers (soaked in water for 30 minutes if using wooden skewers)

Directions:
1. Marinate: In a large bowl, whisk together Greek yogurt, olive oil, lemon juice, oregano, garlic powder, paprika, salt, and pepper. Add chicken cubes and toss to coat evenly. Cover and refrigerate for at least 30 minutes, or up to 4 hours for deeper flavor.
2. Prepare the grill or oven: Preheat your grill to medium-high heat or oven to 400°F (200°C). If using wooden skewers, ensure they are soaked in water for at least 30 minutes before threading the chicken.
3. Assemble the skewers: Thread chicken cubes onto skewers, leaving some space between each piece for even cooking.
4. Cook: Grill the skewers for 10-12 minutes per side, or until cooked through and the internal temperature reaches 165°F (74°C). Alternatively, bake the skewers on a baking sheet lined with parchment paper for 15-20 minutes, flipping halfway through, until cooked through.
5. Serve: Enjoy your chicken skewers immediately with your favorite diabetic-friendly sides, like roasted vegetables, salad, or whole-wheat couscous.

Nutritional Information: Calories: 300, Protein: 35g, Fat: 10g, Carbohydrates: 5g
Sodium: 300mg

Tips:
For a sweeter marinade, add a dash of honey or maple syrup (use sparingly and consider adjusting carbohydrate content accordingly).
Add chopped vegetables like bell peppers, zucchini, or onions to the skewers for additional flavor and nutrients.
Use lean ground pork or beef instead of chicken, adjusting the cooking time as needed.
Experiment with different herbs and spices to personalize the flavor profile.
For a thicker marinade, use full-fat Greek yogurt.

Beef and Vegetable Stir-Fry

Prep Time: 15 minutes | **Cooking Time**: 15 minutes | **Total Time**: 30 minutes | **Serving Size**: 2

Ingredients:
For both variations:
- 1 tablespoon vegetable oil
- 1 clove garlic, minced
- 1 inch ginger, minced
- 1 red bell pepper, thinly sliced
- 1 cup broccoli florets
- 1/2 cup snap peas
- 1/4 cup water chestnuts, sliced (optional)
- 1/4 cup low-sodium soy sauce
- 1 tablespoon cornstarch
- 1/4 cup low-sodium chicken broth
- 1/4 teaspoon sesame oil

For Beef:
- 8 ounces lean beef flank steak, thinly sliced

For Pork:
- 8 ounces lean pork tenderloin, thinly sliced

Directions:
1. Prepare the sauce: In a small bowl, whisk together soy sauce, cornstarch, and chicken broth until smooth.
2. Marinate the meat (optional): Combine the chosen meat with 1 tablespoon soy sauce and 1 tablespoon cornstarch. Marinate for 15 minutes (optional but recommended for tenderness).
3. Heat the oil: In a large skillet or wok, heat vegetable oil over high heat until shimmering.
4. Sauté aromatics: Add garlic and ginger, cook for 30 seconds until fragrant.
5. Stir-fry vegetables: Add bell pepper, broccoli, and snap peas (and water chestnuts if using). Cook for 3-4 minutes, stirring constantly, until vegetables are crisp-tender.
6. Cook the meat: Remove vegetables from the pan and set aside. Add the chosen meat (beef or pork) and cook for 2-3 minutes, stirring frequently, until browned and cooked through.
7. Thicken the sauce: Return the vegetables to the pan. Push everything to the sides and pour in the sauce mixture. Cook for 1-2 minutes, stirring constantly, until the sauce thickens and coats the ingredients.
8. Finish and serve: Stir in sesame oil and serve immediately over cooked brown rice or quinoa for a complete meal.

Nutritional Information: Calories: 350, Carbohydrates: 25g, Fiber: 5g, Net Carbs: 20g, Protein: 30g, Fat: 15g, Sodium: 500mg

Tips:
- Use lean cuts of meat for lower fat content.
- Adjust the amount of soy sauce for desired saltiness.
- Add other low-carb vegetables like zucchini, baby corn, or green beans.
- Substitute tofu or tempeh for a vegetarian option.
- Use low-sodium broth and soy sauce to manage sodium intake.
- Cook rice or quinoa separately and portion control for carbohydrate management.

Zucchini Noodles with Beef Bolognese

Prep Time: 15 minutes | **Cooking Time**: 20 minutes | **Total Time**: 35 minutes | **Serving Size**: 2-3

Ingredients:
For the Zucchini Noodles:
- 2 medium zucchinis
- Spiralizer (or julienne peeler)
- For the Beef Bolognese:
- 1 tablespoon olive oil
- 1/2 onion, diced
- 2 cloves garlic, minced
- 1 celery stalk, diced
- 1 carrot, diced
- 400g lean ground beef
- 1 (28-ounce) can crushed tomatoes
- 1/2 cup beef broth
- 1 tablespoon tomato paste
- 1 teaspoon dried oregano
- 1/2 teaspoon dried basil
- Salt and pepper to taste

For Serving:
- Freshly grated Parmesan cheese (optional)
- Fresh basil leaves (optional)

Directions:
1. Prepare the Zucchini Noodles: Wash and trim the zucchinis. Using a spiralizer or julienne peeler, create long, thin noodles from the zucchini. Set aside.
2. Make the Beef Bolognese: Heat olive oil in a large skillet over medium heat. Add onion, garlic, celery, and carrot, and cook until softened, about 5 minutes.
3. Add ground beef to the pan and cook until browned, breaking it up with a spoon. Drain any excess fat.
4. Stir in crushed tomatoes, beef broth, tomato paste, oregano, and basil. Season with salt and pepper to taste.
5. Bring to a simmer and cook for 15-20 minutes, or until the sauce thickens.
6. While the sauce simmers, cook the zucchini noodles. You can do this in several ways:
7. Microwave: Place the zucchini noodles in a microwave-safe bowl with a tablespoon of water. Microwave on high for 1-2 minutes, or until just tender.
8. Stovetop: Bring a pot of water to a boil. Add the zucchini noodles and cook for 1-2 minutes, or until just tender. Drain immediately.
9. Steaming: Steam the zucchini noodles for 2-3 minutes, or until just tender.
10. Once the sauce and noodles are cooked, combine them in a serving bowl.
11. Garnish with freshly grated Parmesan cheese and fresh basil leaves, if desired.

Nutritional Information: Calories: 350, Carbohydrates: 20g, Fiber: 5g, Protein: 30g, Fat: 15g, Saturated Fat: 5g, Cholesterol: 70mg, Sodium: 400mg

Tips:
- For a richer flavor, use browned ground beef. Simply cook the ground beef in a skillet without oil until browned before adding it to the sauce.
- To make the dish even more diabetic-friendly, use a sugar-free tomato sauce.
- You can also add other vegetables to the Bolognese sauce, such as mushrooms, zucchini, or bell peppers.
- If you don't have a spiralizer, you can use a julienne peeler to create thin strips of zucchini.
- Leftovers can be stored in an airtight container in the refrigerator for up to 3 days.

Mexican Beef Lettuce Wraps

Prep Time: 15 minutes | **Cooking Time**: 20 minutes | **Total Time**: 35 minutes | **Servings**: 4

Ingredients:
- 1 pound lean ground beef (90% lean or higher)
- 1 tablespoon olive oil
- 1 medium onion, diced
- 1 bell pepper (any color), diced
- 2 cloves garlic, minced
- 1 teaspoon chili powder
- 1/2 teaspoon cumin
- 1/4 teaspoon smoked paprika
- 1/4 teaspoon oregano
- 1/4 teaspoon cayenne pepper (optional)
- 1 (14.5-ounce) can diced tomatoes, undrained
- 1/2 cup low-sodium beef broth
- 1/4 cup chopped fresh cilantro
- 1 head romaine lettuce, separated into leaves (washed and dried)
- Optional toppings: shredded cheese, salsa, guacamole, sliced avocado, sour cream, lime wedges

Directions:
1. Prep the vegetables: Dice the onion, bell pepper, and garlic. Wash and dry the romaine lettuce leaves.
2. Cook the beef: Heat olive oil in a large skillet over medium heat. Add the ground beef and cook until browned, breaking it up with a spoon. Drain any excess fat.
3. Add the aromatics: Add the onion, bell pepper, and garlic to the skillet and cook until softened, about 5 minutes.
4. Spice it up: Add the chili powder, cumin, paprika, oregano, and cayenne pepper (if using) to the skillet and cook for 1 minute, stirring constantly, to toast the spices.
5. Simmer and season: Stir in the diced tomatoes, beef broth, and 1/4 cup water. Bring to a simmer and cook for 10 minutes, or until the sauce thickens slightly. Season with salt and pepper to taste.
6. Assemble the wraps: Spoon the beef mixture onto individual romaine lettuce leaves. Top with your desired toppings, such as shredded cheese, salsa, guacamole, sliced avocado, sour cream, and lime wedges.
7. Wrap the lettuce leaves around the filling and enjoy your delicious and diabetes-friendly Mexican meal.

Nutritional Information: Calories: 350, Carbohydrates: 10g, Fiber: 3g, Protein: 30g, Fat: 20g, Saturated Fat: 6g, Cholesterol: 80mg, Sodium: 400mg

Tips:
- Use ground turkey or chicken breast instead of beef for a leaner option.
- Add a can of black beans or kidney beans to the filling for extra protein and fiber.
- Use low-carb tortillas instead of lettuce leaves for a higher carbohydrate option.
- Control portion sizes, especially for toppings like cheese and sour cream.
- Adjust the spices to your preference.
- For a spicier kick, add a chopped jalapeno to the filling.
- Serve with a side of low-carb vegetables, like cauliflower rice or grilled zucchini.

Grilled Pork Tenderloin with Mustard Glaze

Prep Time: 15 minutes | **Cooking Time**: 20-25 minutes | **Total Time**: 35-40 minutes | **Serving Size**: 4

Ingredients:

For the Pork:
- 1 pound pork tenderloin, trimmed of excess fat
- 1 tablespoon olive oil
- 1/2 teaspoon Dijon mustard
- 1/4 teaspoon dried thyme
- 1/4 teaspoon garlic powder
- Salt and pepper to taste

For the Mustard Glaze:
- 1/4 cup Dijon mustard
- 2 tablespoons apple cider vinegar
- 1 tablespoon honey (substitute with 1 tablespoon sugar-free maple syrup)
- 1 tablespoon low-sodium soy sauce
- 1 teaspoon olive oil

Directions:

1. Prepare the pork: In a small bowl, whisk together olive oil, Dijon mustard, thyme, garlic powder, salt, and pepper. Rub the mixture all over the pork tenderloin.
2. Preheat the grill: Preheat your grill to medium-high heat. If using a charcoal grill, let the coals burn down until they are mostly ash.
3. Grill the pork: Place the pork tenderloin on the preheated grill and cook for 10-12 minutes per side, or until the internal temperature reaches 145°F (63°C) as measured with a meat thermometer.
4. Make the glaze: While the pork is cooking, whisk together the Dijon mustard, apple cider vinegar, honey (or sugar-free maple syrup), soy sauce, and olive oil in a small saucepan. Bring the mixture to a simmer over medium heat, then reduce heat and simmer for 5 minutes, or until slightly thickened.
5. Glaze the pork: Brush the pork tenderloin with the glaze during the last 5 minutes of cooking, turning it to coat all sides.
6. Rest and serve: Remove the pork from the grill and let it rest for 5 minutes before slicing. Serve with your favorite diabetic-friendly sides, such as roasted vegetables, grilled asparagus, or a side salad.

Nutritional Information: Calories: 250, Fat: 8g, Carbohydrates: 10g, Sugar: 5g, Protein: 30g, Sodium: 400mg

Tips:
- You can also marinate the pork tenderloin in the olive oil and spice mixture for up to 30 minutes before grilling for added flavor.
- If you don't have a grill, you can bake the pork tenderloin in a preheated oven at 400°F (200°C) for 20-25 minutes, or until it reaches an internal temperature of 145°F (63°C).
- For a beef variation, substitute the pork tenderloin with a lean beef tenderloin and adjust the cooking time accordingly. Beef tenderloin typically cooks a little faster than pork.
- To further reduce the carbohydrate content, use a sugar-free Dijon mustard and omit the glaze entirely.

Baked Pork Chops with Apple Chutney

Prep Time: 15 minutes | **Cooking Time**: 30 minutes | **Total Time**: 45 minutes | **Servings**: 4

Nutritional Information: Calories: 350, Carbohydrates: 25g, Fat: 15g, Protein: 30g, Sodium: 300mg

Ingredients:
For the Pork Chops:
- 4 bone-in, center-cut pork loin chops (1-inch thick)
- 1 tablespoon olive oil
- 1/2 teaspoon garlic powder
- 1/4 teaspoon dried thyme
- 1/4 teaspoon black pepper
- Salt to taste

For the Apple Chutney:
- 2 Granny Smith apples, peeled, cored, and diced
- 1/4 cup chopped onion
- 2 tablespoons apple cider vinegar
- 1 tablespoon olive oil
- 1 teaspoon Dijon mustard
- 1/2 teaspoon ground cinnamon
- 1/4 teaspoon ground ginger
- Pinch of cloves
- Salt and pepper to taste

Directions:
1. Preheat oven to 400°F (200°C).
2. In a small bowl, combine olive oil, garlic powder, thyme, pepper, and salt. Rub the mixture onto the pork chops.
3. Heat a large oven-safe skillet over medium heat. Sear the pork chops for 2-3 minutes per side until golden brown.
4. Transfer the skillet to the preheated oven and bake for 20-25 minutes, or until the pork chops are cooked through and reach an internal temperature of 145°F (63°C).
5. While the pork chops are baking, prepare the chutney. In a saucepan, heat olive oil over medium heat. Add onions and cook until softened, about 5 minutes.
6. Add apples, vinegar, mustard, cinnamon, ginger, cloves, salt, and pepper. Bring to a simmer and cook for 10-15 minutes, stirring occasionally, until the apples are softened and the chutney thickens slightly.
7. Serve the pork chops topped with the apple chutney.

Pork and Vegetable Stir-Fry

Prep Time: 15 minutes | **Cooking Time**: 10 minutes | **Total Time**: 25 minutes | **Servings**: 4

Ingredients:

For the marinade (both options):
- 2 tbsp. low-sodium soy sauce
- 1 tbsp. rice vinegar
- 1 tsp. cornstarch
- 1/2 tsp. grated ginger
- 1 clove garlic, minced
- 1/4 tsp. black pepper

For the pork stir-fry:
- 12 oz. lean pork loin, thinly sliced
- 1 tbsp. vegetable oil
- 1 red bell pepper, sliced
- 1 cup broccoli florets
- 1/2 cup snap peas
- 1/4 cup sliced green onions
- 1/4 cup low-sodium chicken broth

For the beef stir-fry:
- 12 oz. lean flank steak, thinly sliced
- 1 tbsp. vegetable oil
- 1 cup snow peas
- 1 cup baby carrots, sliced
- 1/2 cup sliced mushrooms
- 1/4 cup sliced green onions
- 1/4 cup low-sodium beef broth

Directions:
1. Marinate: In a bowl, whisk together marinade ingredients. Add pork or beef and marinate for 15 minutes.
2. Heat oil: Heat oil in a large skillet or wok over high heat.
3. Cook protein: Add pork or beef and cook until browned and cooked through (3-4 minutes). Remove from pan and set aside.
4. Sauté vegetables: Add bell pepper (pork) or snow peas (beef) and cook for 1-2 minutes. Add remaining vegetables and cook for another 2-3 minutes, until tender-crisp.
5. Return protein: Return pork or beef to the pan and toss with vegetables.
6. Add broth: Pour in broth (chicken or beef, depending on protein) and simmer for 1 minute.
7. Thicken sauce (optional): Mix 1 tbsp. cornstarch with 1 tbsp. water to form a slurry. Add to the pan and stir until sauce thickens slightly.
8. Garnish and serve: Garnish with green onions and serve immediately.

Nutritional Information: Calories: 300 (pork) / 320 (beef), Carbohydrates: 15g (pork) / 10g (beef), Fiber: 5g, Protein: 30g (pork) / 35g (beef), Fat: 10g (pork) / 15g (beef)

Tips:
- Use non-starchy vegetables like broccoli, bell peppers, and mushrooms for a lower-carb option.
- Substitute brown rice or quinoa for a healthier carbohydrate source.
- Opt for low-sodium soy sauce and chicken/beef broth to manage sodium intake.
- Adjust the amount of cornstarch in the sauce for desired thickness.
- Experiment with different vegetables and spices to customize the flavor profile.

Pork and Spinach Stuffed Mushrooms

Prep Time: 15 minutes | **Cooking Time**: 25 minutes | **Total Time**: 40 minutes | **Servings**: 4

Ingredients:
- 8 large Portobello mushrooms, cleaned and stems removed
- 1 tablespoon olive oil
- 1/2 onion, finely chopped
- 2 cloves garlic, minced
- 1/2 pound lean ground beef (90% lean or higher)
- 1/4 cup chopped fresh parsley
- 1/4 cup chopped fresh dill
- 1/2 teaspoon dried thyme
- 1/4 teaspoon black pepper
- 1/4 cup low-sodium chicken broth
- 4 ounces fresh spinach, chopped
- 1/4 cup crumbled feta cheese (optional)

Directions:
1. Preheat oven to 400°F (200°C). Line a baking sheet with parchment paper.
2. In a large skillet, heat olive oil over medium heat. Add onion and cook until softened, about 5 minutes. Add garlic and cook for another minute.
3. Crumble in ground beef and cook until browned, breaking it up with a spoon. Drain any excess fat.
4. Stir in parsley, dill, thyme, and pepper. Cook for another minute until fragrant.
5. Add chicken broth and bring to a simmer. Scrape up any browned bits from the bottom of the pan.
6. Stir in spinach and cook until wilted. Remove from heat and stir in feta cheese, if using.
7. Divide the mushroom filling evenly among the Portobello mushroom caps. Arrange filled mushrooms on the prepared baking sheet.
8. Bake for 20-25 minutes, or until mushrooms are tender and filling is cooked through.
9. Serve immediately.

Nutritional Information: Calories: 250, Total Fat: 8g, Saturated Fat: 3g, Cholesterol: 50mg, Sodium: 300mg, Carbohydrates: 10g, Fiber: 2g, Sugar: 3g, Protein: 25g

Tips:
- For a vegetarian option, replace ground beef with crumbled tofu or lentils.
- You can also use other low-fat cheeses, such as ricotta or mozzarella, in place of feta cheese.
- To make this recipe ahead of time, prepare the filling and stuff the mushrooms. Store them in the refrigerator for up to 24 hours before baking.
- Serve with a side of roasted vegetables or whole-wheat couscous for a complete meal.

Beef and Broccoli Stir-Fry

Prep Time: 10 minutes | **Cooking Time**: 15 minutes | **Total Time**: 25 minutes | **Servings**: 4

Ingredients:

- 1 pound flank steak, thinly sliced
- 1 tablespoon cornstarch
- 1 tablespoon soy sauce (low-sodium)
- 1 teaspoon sesame oil
- 1/2 teaspoon ginger, minced
- 1 head broccoli, cut into florets
- 1 red bell pepper, sliced
- 1/2 cup water
- 1 tablespoon cornstarch (mixed with 2 tablespoons water)
- Salt and pepper to taste

Directions:

1. In a bowl, combine sliced beef, cornstarch, soy sauce, sesame oil, and ginger. Toss to coat.
2. Heat a large skillet or wok over high heat. Add a tablespoon of oil and stir-fry the beef for 2-3 minutes until browned. Remove from the pan and set aside.
3. Add another tablespoon of oil to the pan and stir-fry the broccoli and bell pepper for 5 minutes, or until tender-crisp.
4. Return the beef to the pan with the water. Bring to a simmer and cook for 1 minute.
5. Stir in the cornstarch mixture and cook until the sauce thickens slightly.
6. Season with salt and pepper to taste.

Nutritional Information: Calories: 250, Carbohydrates: 15g, Fat: 10g, Protein: 25g, Sodium: 500mg

Tips:

- For both recipes, use low-sodium ingredients whenever possible.
- You can adjust the amount of spices and herbs to your liking.
- Serve the pork chops with a side of roasted vegetables or brown rice for a complete meal.
- Serve the beef stir-fry with cauliflower rice or quinoa for a low-carb option.

MEAL PLAN

DAY 1:
Breakfast: Greek Yogurt Parfait
Lunch: Grilled Chicken Salad
Dinner: Grilled Chicken Breast with Roasted Vegetables

DAY 2:
Breakfast: Oatmeal with Fresh Fruit
Lunch: Quinoa and Black Bean Bowl
Dinner: Salmon and Asparagus Foil Packets

DAY 3:
Breakfast: Vegetable Omelette
Lunch: Salmon and Vegetable Stir-Fry
Dinner: Vegetarian Quinoa Stir-Fry

DAY 4:
Breakfast: Whole Grain Toast with Avocado
Lunch: Turkey and Hummus Wrap
Dinner: Turkey and Vegetable Skewers

DAY 5:
Breakfast: Cottage Cheese and Pineapple Bowl
Lunch: Mediterranean Chickpea Salad
Dinner: Cauliflower Fried Rice with Shrimp

DAY 6:
Breakfast: Chia Seed Pudding
Lunch: Vegetable and Tofu Stir-Fry
Dinner: Lemon Herb Baked Cod with Sweet Potato Mash

DAY 7:
Breakfast: Quinoa Breakfast Bowl
Lunch: Caprese Chicken Salad
Dinner: Chickpea and Spinach Curry

DAY 8:
Breakfast: Smoothie Bowl
Lunch: Whole Wheat Pasta with Pesto and Vegetables
Dinner: Stuffed Bell Peppers with Ground Turkey

DAY 9:
Breakfast: Egg and Vegetable Wrap
Lunch: Shrimp and Avocado Lettuce Wraps
Dinner: Eggplant and Zucchini Lasagna

DAY 10:
Breakfast: Sweet Potato Hash
Lunch: Stuffed Bell Peppers
Dinner: Beef and Vegetable Stir-Fry with Brown Rice

Repeat the breakfast, lunch, and dinner options.

DINING OUT

Plan Ahead:
- Review the restaurant menu online if possible.
- Choose a restaurant that offers a variety of healthier options.

Control Portions:
- Opt for smaller portions or consider sharing a dish.
- Ask for a to-go box at the beginning and save part of your meal for later.

Choose Wisely:
- Select lean proteins like grilled chicken or fish.
- Opt for dishes that are baked, grilled, steamed, or roasted instead of fried.

Skip Sugary Drinks:
- Choose water, unsweetened tea, or sparkling water instead of sugary beverages.
- Limit alcohol intake and opt for lighter options.

Watch Hidden Sugars:
- Be cautious of sauces, dressings, and marinades that may contain hidden sugars.
- Ask for sauces on the side to control the amount you use.

Emphasize Vegetables:
- Include plenty of non-starchy vegetables in your meal.
- Request double vegetables or a side salad instead of high-carb sides.

Manage Carbohydrates:
- Control portions of carbohydrates like rice, pasta, or bread.
- Choose whole grains when available.

Communicate Dietary Needs:
- Inform your server about your dietary preferences and restrictions.
- Don't hesitate to ask for modifications to meet your needs.

Be Mindful of Desserts:
- Share a dessert or opt for a smaller portion.
- Consider fruit-based desserts or those with sugar substitutes.

SOCIAL GATHERINGS

Eat Before the Event:
- Have a balanced meal or snack before attending social events to curb hunger.

Bring a Dish:
- Contribute a diabetes-friendly dish to share.
- Ensure there are healthier options available.

Stay Active:
- Engage in conversation, participate in activities, or take a walk to manage blood sugar levels.

Mindful Alcohol Consumption:
- Limit alcohol intake and choose lighter options.
- Stay hydrated with water between alcoholic beverages.

Stay Hydrated:
- Drink water throughout the event to stay hydrated.
- Limit sugary beverages and choose alternatives like sparkling water.

Monitor Blood Sugar:
- Regularly check your blood sugar levels, especially if the event involves changes to your routine.

Resist Peer Pressure:
- Politely decline unhealthy food offerings if they don't align with your dietary goals.
- Focus on enjoying the company rather than overindulging in food.

Be Prepared:
- Carry snacks like nuts, seeds, or fresh fruit in case healthy options are limited.

Educate Others:
- Share your dietary needs with friends and family, so they understand and can support your choices.

Enjoy in Moderation:
- Allow yourself to enjoy treats in moderation without feeling deprived.
- Focus on the overall balance of your meals and snacks.

THANKSGIVING DINNER MENU

Roasted Vegetable Platter with Yogurt Dip

Prep Time: 15 minutes | **Cooking Time**: 30 minutes | **Total Time**: 45 minutes | **Serving Size**: 6-8 servings

Ingredients:
- 1 tablespoon olive oil
- 1 red bell pepper, sliced
- 1 yellow bell pepper, sliced
- 1 orange bell pepper, sliced
- 1 red onion, sliced
- 1 zucchini, sliced
- 1 eggplant, sliced
- 1/2 cup cherry tomatoes
- 1/4 cup crumbled feta cheese (optional)
- Fresh herbs (thyme, rosemary, parsley), for garnish
- For the Yogurt Dip:
- 1 cup plain Greek yogurt
- 1/4 cup chopped fresh dill
- 1 tablespoon lemon juice
- 1/2 teaspoon garlic powder
- 1/4 teaspoon salt
- Pinch of black pepper

Directions:
1. Preheat oven to 400°F (200°C). Line a baking sheet with parchment paper.
2. In a large bowl, toss vegetables with olive oil, salt, and pepper. Spread vegetables evenly on the prepared baking sheet.
3. Roast for 20-25 minutes, or until vegetables are tender and slightly browned.
4. While the vegetables are roasting, prepare the yogurt dip. In a small bowl, whisk together yogurt, dill, lemon juice, garlic powder, salt, and pepper. Taste and adjust seasonings as needed.
5. Once the vegetables are roasted, remove them from the oven and let them cool slightly. Arrange vegetables on a platter and top with crumbled feta cheese (optional) and fresh herbs.
6. Serve with the yogurt dip on the side.

Nutritional Information: Calories: 150, Carbohydrates: 15g, Fiber: 5g, Sugar: 8g, Fat: 5g, Protein: 2g

Tips:
- For a more flavorful dip, you can add a grated clove of garlic or a pinch of red pepper flakes to the yogurt mixture.
- If you don't have fresh herbs, you can use 1 teaspoon of dried herbs instead.
- You can substitute any of the vegetables in this recipe with your favorites. Just be sure to adjust the cooking time accordingly.
- To make this dish vegan, omit the feta cheese and use a vegan yogurt for the dip.

Herb-Roasted Turkey Breast

Prep Time: 20 minutes | **Cooking Time**: 1.5 - 2 hours | **Total Time**: 1.5 - 2.2 hours | **Serving Size**: 4-6

Ingredients:
- 1 (3-4 lbs.) bone-in, skin-on turkey breast
- 2 tablespoons olive oil
- 1 tablespoon chopped fresh rosemary
- 1 tablespoon chopped fresh thyme
- 1/2 teaspoon dried sage
- 1/4 teaspoon garlic powder
- 1/4 teaspoon onion powder
- 1/4 teaspoon black pepper
- 1/2 teaspoon salt (or less, to taste)
- 1 lemon, sliced
- 1 onion, quartered
- 2 carrots, chopped (optional)
- 1 cup low-sodium chicken broth

Directions:
1. Preheat oven to 425°F (220°C). Remove giblets and neck from the turkey cavity and discard. Rinse the turkey breast and pat it dry with paper towels.
2. Prepare the herb rub: In a small bowl, combine olive oil, rosemary, thyme, sage, garlic powder, onion powder, pepper, and salt.
3. Loosen the skin: Carefully loosen the skin over the breast meat using your fingers, creating a pocket without tearing the skin. Rub half of the herb mixture under the skin. Season the cavity with salt and pepper.
4. Stuff and truss: Place lemon slices and onion wedges in the cavity. Tie the legs together with kitchen twine to help retain moisture.
5. Brush and season: Brush the remaining herb mixture over the skin of the turkey breast. Season the outside with additional salt and pepper, to taste.
6. Roast: Place the turkey breast in a roasting pan, breast-side up. Add chopped carrots around the pan (optional). Pour chicken broth into the bottom of the pan.
7. Basting and cooking: Roast the turkey for 1 hour, basting with pan juices every 20 minutes. Reduce the oven temperature to 375°F (190°C) and continue roasting for another 30-45 minutes, or until an instant-read thermometer inserted into the thickest part of the thigh (not touching bone) reaches 165°F (74°C).
8. Rest and tent: Remove the turkey from the oven and tent it loosely with foil. Let it rest for 15-20 minutes before carving. This allows the juices to redistribute, resulting in moist and flavorful meat.
9. Discard the skin before carving and slicing the turkey. Serve with roasted vegetables and your favorite diabetic-friendly sides.

Nutritional Information: Calories: 300, Carbohydrates: 2g, Protein: 35g, Fat: 15g, Sodium: 300mg

Tips:
- For extra flavor, add a few cloves of garlic under the skin along with the herbs.
- If the skin starts to brown too quickly, tent it loosely with foil during the last part of cooking.
- Use low-sodium or no-sodium broth for added sodium control.
- To control portion sizes, weigh the cooked turkey and divide it evenly among guests.
- Leftovers can be stored in the refrigerator for up to 3 days or frozen for longer storage.

Quinoa and Cranberry Stuffed Acorn Squash

Prep Time: 15 minutes | **Cooking Time**: 50 minutes | **Total Time**: 65 minutes | **Servings**: 4

Ingredients:
- 2 medium acorn squash
- 1 tablespoon olive oil
- 1/2 cup uncooked quinoa, rinsed
- 1 cup vegetable broth
- 1/4 cup chopped onion
- 2 cloves garlic, minced
- 1/2 teaspoon dried thyme
- 1/4 teaspoon ground cinnamon
- 1/4 teaspoon black pepper
- 1/4 cup dried cranberries
- 1/4 cup chopped pecans, toasted (optional)
- Salt and pepper to taste

Directions:
1. Preheat oven to 400°F (200°C). Line a baking sheet with parchment paper.
2. Cut the squash in half lengthwise and remove the seeds. Brush the flesh of the squash with olive oil and season with salt and pepper. Place the squash halves flesh-side down on the prepared baking sheet.
3. Bake for 30 minutes, or until the squash is tender.
4. While the squash is baking, cook the quinoa. In a pot, combine the quinoa, vegetable broth, and 1/4 teaspoon salt. Bring to a boil, then reduce heat, cover, and simmer for 15 minutes, or until the quinoa is cooked and fluffy.
5. In a skillet, heat 1 tablespoon of olive oil over medium heat. Add the onion and cook until softened, about 5 minutes. Add the garlic, thyme, cinnamon, and black pepper, and cook for 1 minute more.
6. Stir in the cooked quinoa and cranberries. Heat through for a few minutes.
7. Once the squash is cooked, remove it from the oven and flip it over. Fill each squash half with the quinoa mixture. Sprinkle with toasted pecans, if using.
8. Bake for an additional 15-20 minutes, or until the squash is golden brown and the filling is heated through. Serve immediately.

Nutritional Information: Calories: 350, Carbohydrates: 45g, Fiber: 8g, Protein: 12g, Fat: 10g, Sugar: 10g

Tips:
- To test if the squash is done, pierce it with a fork. It should be tender but not mushy.
- You can substitute other chopped nuts for the pecans, such as walnuts or almonds.
- For a vegan option, omit the pecans and use vegetable broth instead of chicken broth.
- Serve with a side of roasted vegetables or a small green salad for a complete and balanced meal.
- This recipe can be easily doubled or tripled to feed a larger crowd.

Green Bean Almondine

Prep Time: 10 minutes | **Cooking Time**: 15 minutes | **Total Time**: 25 minutes | **Serving Size**: 4 servings

Ingredients:
- 1 pound fresh green beans, trimmed
- 1 tablespoon olive oil
- 1/4 cup sliced almonds
- 1 shallot, thinly sliced
- 1 garlic clove, minced
- 1/4 teaspoon dried thyme
- 1/4 teaspoon dried parsley
- Salt and freshly ground black pepper to taste
- 1/4 cup vegetable broth
- 2 tablespoons lemon juice
- 1 tablespoon chopped fresh parsley (optional, for garnish)

Directions:
1. Prep the green beans: Wash and trim the green beans. You can leave them whole or blanch them for 2-3 minutes in boiling water for a brighter green color and slightly softer texture. Drain and immediately immerse in ice water to stop the cooking process.
2. Toast the almonds: Heat olive oil in a large skillet over medium heat. Add the almonds and cook, stirring frequently, until golden brown and fragrant, about 3-4 minutes. Transfer the almonds to a plate and set aside.
3. Sauté the aromatics: In the same skillet, add the shallot and cook for 2-3 minutes until softened. Add the garlic, thyme, and parsley and cook for another minute, stirring constantly.
4. Cook the green beans: Add the green beans to the skillet and saute for 3-5 minutes, stirring occasionally, until crisp-tender.
5. Deglaze and season: Pour in the vegetable broth and lemon juice. Season with salt and pepper to taste. Bring to a simmer and cook for another minute, or until the broth thickens slightly.
6. Serve: Remove from heat and stir in the toasted almonds. Garnish with fresh parsley, if desired.

Nutritional information: Calories: 150, Carbohydrates: 15g, Dietary fiber: 4g, Net carbs: 11g, Fat: 8g, Protein: 3g

Tips:
- For added flavor, you can substitute the vegetable broth with low-sodium chicken broth.
- If you prefer a sweeter dish, add a sprinkle of stevia or a 1/4 teaspoon of sugar-free maple syrup to the broth.
- This recipe is easily adaptable to other vegetables like broccoli, asparagus, or zucchini.
- Serve alongside other diabetes-friendly dishes like roasted turkey breast, roasted sweet potatoes, or quinoa salad for a complete and balanced Thanksgiving meal.

Mashed Cauliflower

Prep Time: 10 minutes | **Cooking Time**: 15 minutes | **Total Time**: 25 minutes | **Serving Size**: 4-6

Ingredients:
- 1 head cauliflower, florets removed and chopped
- 1/4 cup unsweetened almond milk or vegetable broth
- 2 tablespoons unsalted butter, ghee, or olive oil
- 2 cloves garlic, minced
- 1/4 cup grated Parmesan cheese (optional)
- 1/4 cup chopped fresh herbs (parsley, chives, dill, or thyme)
- Salt and pepper to taste

Directions:
1. Steam or boil the cauliflower: Place the chopped cauliflower florets in a steamer basket or pot with a few inches of water. Bring to a boil, then reduce heat and steam for 10-12 minutes, or until tender. Alternatively, boil the cauliflower florets in unsalted water for 8-10 minutes. Drain well and set aside.
2. Mash the cauliflower: Transfer the cooked cauliflower to a large bowl or food processor. Add the almond milk or broth and 1 tablespoon of the butter or oil. Mash with a potato masher or blend until smooth and creamy. You can leave some texture if desired.
3. Season and flavor: Add the remaining butter or oil, garlic, Parmesan cheese (if using), herbs, salt, and pepper. Taste and adjust seasonings as needed.
4. Serve warm: Enjoy your mashed cauliflower immediately as a side dish for your Thanksgiving meal.

Nutritional Information: Calories: 120, Carbohydrates: 9g, Fiber: 3g, Net Carbs: 6g, Fat: 7g, Protein: 4g, Vitamin C: 70% DV, Potassium: 10% DV

Tips:
- For an extra creamy texture, add a tablespoon of cream cheese or sour cream with the milk or broth.
- Roast the cauliflower florets instead of steaming or boiling for a deeper flavor. Simply toss them with olive oil, salt, and pepper, and roast at 400°F for 20-25 minutes, until tender and slightly browned.
- Get creative with different herbs and spices to personalize the flavor. Try adding paprika, turmeric, nutritional yeast, or a dash of nutmeg.
- Make it ahead of time: Prepare the mashed cauliflower up to 2 days in advance and store it in an airtight container in the refrigerator. Reheat gently on the stovetop or in the microwave before serving.

Pumpkin Chia Pudding Parfait

Prep Time: 10 minutes **Cooking Time**: N/A | **Total Time**: 10 minutes | **Serving Size**: 2

Ingredients:
- 1/2 cup unsweetened almond milk or low-fat milk
- 1/4 cup canned pumpkin puree
- 2 tablespoons chia seeds
- 1/2 teaspoon pumpkin pie spice
- 1/4 teaspoon ground cinnamon
- 1/4 teaspoon ground ginger
- Pinch of nutmeg
- 1 tablespoon pure maple syrup, or to taste
- 1/4 cup plain Greek yogurt
- 1/4 cup chopped pecans or walnuts
- Fresh cranberries, for garnish (optional)

Directions:
1. In a medium bowl, whisk together almond milk, pumpkin puree, chia seeds, spices, and maple syrup until well combined. Ensure no chia seed clumps remain.
2. Cover the bowl and refrigerate for at least 4 hours, or overnight, to allow the chia seeds to thicken and absorb the liquid.
3. When ready to serve, assemble the parfaits. Divide the chia pudding evenly between two glasses or parfait cups.
4. Top each layer with 1/2 of the Greek yogurt and sprinkle with chopped nuts.
5. Garnish with fresh cranberries, if desired.

Nutritional Information: Calories: 340, Carbohydrates: 30g, Fiber: 10g, Net Carbs: 20g, Protein: 10g, Fat: 18g

Tips:
- For a thicker pudding, use less milk or more chia seeds.
- Adjust the sweetness to your preference. You can use other natural sweeteners like stevia or monk fruit extract instead of maple syrup.
- Get creative with the toppings! Try using chopped apple, granola, or a drizzle of sugar-free caramel sauce.
- Prepare the chia pudding in advance for a quick and easy grab-and-go dessert. It will keep well in the refrigerator for up to 3 days.

CHRISTMAS DINNER MENU

Smoked Salmon Cucumber Bites

Prep Time: 10 minutes | **Cooking Time**: N/A | **Total Time**: 10 minutes | **Servings**: 24

Ingredients:

- 1 large cucumber, washed and ends trimmed
- 4 oz. (113g) cold-smoked salmon, thinly sliced
- 4 oz. (113g) light cream cheese
- 1/4 cup fresh dill, chopped (plus extra sprigs for garnish)
- 1 tsp. lemon zest
- 1 tsp. lemon juice
- Freshly ground black pepper

Directions:

1. Slice the cucumber: Wash and dry the cucumber. Cut off the ends and discard. Slice the cucumber into 24 rounds, about 1/4 inch thick.
2. Prepare the cream cheese mixture: In a medium bowl, combine the light cream cheese, chopped dill, lemon zest, lemon juice, and black pepper. Mix well until smooth and spreadable.
3. Assemble the bites: Spread about 1 teaspoon of the cream cheese mixture onto each cucumber round. Top each with a piece of smoked salmon.
4. Garnish and serve: Garnish each bite with a fresh dill sprig. Arrange the bites on a platter and serve immediately.

Nutritional Information: Calories: 90, Carbohydrates: 3g, Protein: 8g, Fat: 5g, Sodium: 180mg

Tips:

- For a richer flavor, use full-fat cream cheese. However, keep in mind that this will increase the calorie and fat content per serving.
- To reduce the sodium content, use low-sodium cream cheese and smoked salmon.
- If you don't have fresh dill, you can use 1/2 teaspoon dried dill.
- For a festive touch, use cookie cutters to cut the cucumber slices into star or Christmas tree shapes.
- Serve these bites with a dollop of low-fat Greek yogurt or sour cream for an extra protein boost.

Balsamic Glazed Roast Beef

Prep Time: 15 minutes | **Cooking Time**: 1 hour 30 minutes 2 hours | **Total Time**: 1 hour 45 minutes - 2 hours 15 minutes | **Serving Size**: 6-8 people

Ingredients:
- 2-3 lbs. lean beef roast (eye round, top sirloin, or rump roast)
- 1 tablespoon olive oil
- 1 teaspoon dried thyme
- 1/2 teaspoon dried rosemary
- 1/2 teaspoon onion powder
- 1/4 teaspoon black pepper
- 1/2 cup low-sodium beef broth
- 1/4 cup balsamic vinegar
- 1 tablespoon Dijon mustard
- 1 tablespoon sugar substitute (such as stevia or erythritol)
- 1/4 teaspoon cornstarch (optional, for thickening)

Directions:
1. Preheat oven to 325°F (165°C).
2. Pat the roast dry with paper towels. In a small bowl, combine olive oil, thyme, rosemary, onion powder, and black pepper. Rub the spice mixture evenly over the roast.
3. Place the roast in a roasting pan. Pour in the beef broth.
4. Roast the beef for 1 hour 15 minutes to 1 hour 30 minutes per pound, or until it reaches an internal temperature of 145°F (63°C) for medium-rare, 160°F (71°C) for medium, or 170°F (77°C) for well-done.
5. While the roast cooks, prepare the glaze. In a small saucepan, combine balsamic vinegar, Dijon mustard, and sugar substitute. Bring to a simmer over medium heat and cook for 5-7 minutes, or until slightly thickened. If desired, whisk in cornstarch mixed with 1 tablespoon water to further thicken the glaze.
6. Remove the roast from the oven and tent with foil. Let it rest for 10-15 minutes.
7. Slice the roast thinly. Transfer the slices to a serving platter and spoon the balsamic glaze over the top.

Nutritional Information: Calories: 350, Protein: 35g, Fat: 15g, Saturated fat: 4g, Carbohydrates: 25g, Sugar 5g, Sodium: 300mg

Tips:
- Choose a lean cut of beef with little visible fat.
- Use low-sodium beef broth and Dijon mustard to keep sodium content in check.
- Sugar substitutes can vary in sweetness, so adjust the amount to your taste.
- For a thicker glaze, add the cornstarch slurry gradually, whisking constantly until desired consistency is reached.
- Serve the roast with roasted vegetables, such as broccoli, carrots, or Brussels sprouts.
- Be sure to monitor your blood sugar levels before and after consuming this dish, especially if you are new to managing diabetes.

Herb-Roasted Brussels sprouts

Prep Time: 10 minutes | **Cooking Time**: 20-25 minutes | **Total Time**: 30-35 minutes | Serving Size: 4-6

Ingredients:

- 1 pound Brussels sprouts, trimmed and halved
- 1 tablespoon olive oil
- 1/2 teaspoon dried thyme
- 1/4 teaspoon dried rosemary
- 1/4 teaspoon garlic powder
- Salt and black pepper to taste
- Optional: 1/4 cup chopped pecans or walnuts, toasted

Directions:

1. Preheat oven to 400°F (200°C). Line a baking sheet with parchment paper.
2. In a large bowl, toss Brussels sprouts with olive oil, thyme, rosemary, garlic powder, salt, and pepper.
3. Spread Brussels sprouts evenly on the prepared baking sheet.
4. Roast for 20-25 minutes, or until Brussels sprouts are tender and slightly browned, flipping halfway through.
5. Remove from oven and serve immediately.
6. Optionally, garnish with toasted pecans or walnuts for added crunch.

Nutritional Information: Calories: 70, Carbohydrates: 10g, Fiber: 3g, Sugar: 5g, Protein: 2g, Fat: 4g

Tips:

- For a sweeter flavor, drizzle the roasted Brussels sprouts with a balsamic glaze or maple syrup.
- If you don't have fresh herbs, you can use 1/2 teaspoon each of dried thyme and rosemary.
- Make sure to not overcrowd the baking sheet, as this will prevent the Brussels sprouts from roasting evenly.
- You can test the doneness of the Brussels sprouts by piercing them with a fork. They should be tender but not mushy.

Cauliflower and Broccoli Gratin

Prep Time: 15 minutes | **Cooking Time**: 30 minutes | **Total Time**: 45 minutes | **Servings**: 4-6

Ingredients:

- 1 head cauliflower, cut into florets
- 1 head broccoli, cut into florets
- 1 tablespoon olive oil
- 1/2 onion, diced
- 2 cloves garlic, minced
- 1/4 cup all-purpose flour (whole wheat flour can be substituted)
- 1 cup low-fat milk
- 1/2 cup plain Greek yogurt
- 1/2 cup grated Gruyere cheese
- 1/4 cup grated Parmesan cheese
- 1/4 teaspoon nutmeg
- Salt and pepper to taste
- 1/4 cup breadcrumbs

Directions:

1. Preheat oven to 375°F (190°C). Lightly grease a baking dish.
2. Steam or boil the cauliflower and broccoli florets until tender-crisp, about 5-7 minutes. Drain and set aside.
3. Heat olive oil in a skillet over medium heat. Add onion and cook until softened, about 5 minutes. Add garlic and cook for another minute.
4. Sprinkle flour over the onion and garlic, and cook for 1 minute, stirring constantly. Slowly whisk in milk until a smooth sauce forms. Bring to a simmer and cook for 2 minutes, stirring frequently.
5. Remove from heat and stir in yogurt, Gruyere cheese, Parmesan cheese, nutmeg, salt, and pepper.
6. Combine the cooked vegetables and cheese sauce in the prepared baking dish.
7. Sprinkle breadcrumbs on top.
8. Bake for 20-25 minutes, or until golden brown and bubbly.
9. Let cool slightly before serving.

Nutritional Information: Calories: 250, Carbohydrates: 25g, Fiber: 5g, Protein: 15g, Fat: 10g, Saturated Fat: 5g, Sodium: 300mg

Tips:

- To reduce carbohydrates further, use half cauliflower and half zucchini noodles.
- For a richer flavor, use a blend of low-fat mozzarella and sharp cheddar cheese instead of Gruyere.
- Serve with a side of grilled chicken or fish for a complete meal.
- This gratin can be prepared ahead of time and reheated in the oven before serving.

Spinach and Pomegranate Salad

Prep Time: 10 minutes | **Cooking Time**: None | **Total Time**: 10 minutes | **Servings**: 4

Ingredients:
- 4 cups baby spinach
- 1 cup halved red seedless grapes
- 1/2 cup crumbled feta cheese
- 1/4 cup pomegranate arils
- 1/4 cup chopped walnuts
- 2 tablespoons olive oil
- 1 tablespoon red wine vinegar
- 1/2 teaspoon Dijon mustard
- 1/4 teaspoon dried oregano
- Salt and pepper to taste

Directions:
1. Wash and dry the spinach: Thoroughly rinse the spinach and pat it dry with a salad spinner or paper towels.
2. Prepare the other ingredients: Halve the grapes, crumble the feta cheese, and chop the walnuts.
3. Make the dressing: In a small bowl, whisk together the olive oil, red wine vinegar, Dijon mustard, oregano, salt, and pepper.
4. Assemble the salad: In a large bowl, combine the spinach, grapes, feta cheese, pomegranate arils, and walnuts. Toss gently to combine.
5. Dress the salad: Drizzle the dressing over the salad and toss again to coat evenly.
6. Serve immediately: Enjoy this refreshing and nutritious salad as a side dish or light lunch.

Nutritional Information: Calories: 150, Carbohydrates: 15g, Fiber: 4g, Sugar: 8g, Fat: 5g, Protein: 3g

Tips:
- For a richer flavor, toast the walnuts in a dry skillet over medium heat for a few minutes before adding them to the salad.
- If you don't have red wine vinegar, you can substitute another type of vinegar, such as balsamic or apple cider vinegar.
- To make the salad ahead of time, prepare all the ingredients and store them separately in the refrigerator. Assemble and dress the salad just before serving.
- For a vegan option, omit the feta cheese or use a vegan alternative.

Sugar-Free Berry Trifle

Prep Time: 15 minutes | **Cooking Time**: 20 minutes | **Total Time**: 35 minutes | **Servings**: 6-8

Ingredients:
For the Jelly:
- 1 packet sugar-free jelly crystals (any flavor you like)
- 400ml boiling water
- 1 tbsp. chia seeds (optional)

For the Custard:
- 300ml unsweetened almond milk
- 2 egg yolks
- 1 tbsp. cornstarch
- 1/2 tsp. vanilla extract
- 1/4 cup sugar-free sweetener (stevia, erythritol, etc.)

For the Trifle:
- 250g mixed berries (fresh or frozen)
- 100g sugar-free sponge fingers (optional)
- 200ml whipped double cream (low-fat or sugar-free alternative)
- Fresh berries for garnish

Directions:
1. Prepare the Jelly: Dissolve the jelly crystals in boiling water according to package instructions. Stir in the chia seeds (if using) and pour into a shallow dish. Refrigerate for at least 2 hours until set.
2. Make the Custard: In a saucepan, whisk together almond milk, egg yolks, cornstarch, and vanilla extract. Cook over medium heat, whisking constantly, until thickened and simmering. Remove from heat and stir in sweetener. Pour into a bowl and cover with plastic wrap directly on the surface to prevent a skin from forming. Refrigerate for at least 30 minutes until chilled.
3. Assemble the Trifle: Break the sponge fingers (if using) into pieces. In a serving dish, layer half the jelly, followed by half the berries. Top with half the sponge fingers (if using) and half the chilled custard. Repeat with another layer of jelly, berries, sponge fingers (if using), and custard.
4. Top and Chill: Dollop with whipped cream and garnish with fresh berries. Refrigerate for at least 1 hour before serving.

Nutritional Information: Calories: 250, Carbohydrates: 25g, Fat: 10g, Protein: 5g, Fiber: 3g

Tips:
- For a richer flavor, use unsweetened full-fat cream for the whipped cream.
- Substitute the sponge fingers with angel food cake pieces or low-carb cookies.
- Use different types of berries for added variety and flavor.
- Serve the trifle in individual glasses for a more elegant presentation.
- If you prefer a firmer custard, use 1 tablespoon of cornstarch instead of 1/2 tablespoon.
- Remember to adjust the sweetener quantity based on your preferred sweetness and the specific sweetener you use.

BIRTHDAY CELEBRATION MENU

Caprese Skewers

Prep Time: 10 minutes | **Cooking Time**: 0 minutes | Total Time: 10 minutes | **Serving Size**: 12

Ingredients:

- 12 cherry tomatoes, halved
- 12 mozzarella cheese balls (bocconcini or ciliegine), halved
- 12 fresh basil leaves
- 12 thin slices of prosciutto (optional)
- Extra virgin olive oil
- Balsamic glaze (optional)
- Skewers

Directions:

1. Assemble the skewers: Thread a cherry tomato half, mozzarella cheese ball half, and basil leaf onto each skewer.
2. Wrap with prosciutto (optional): If using prosciutto, gently wrap each skewer with a slice of prosciutto, tucking the ends under the other ingredients.
3. Drizzle and garnish (optional): You can lightly drizzle the skewers with olive oil and balsamic glaze for added flavor and shine.
4. Serve: These skewers are best enjoyed fresh. If desired, you can grill them briefly for a slightly smoky flavor. Heat a grill pan or grill to medium heat and cook the skewers for 1-2 minutes per side, until the cheese starts to soften slightly.

Nutritional Information: Calories: 100, Carbohydrates: 8g, Fiber: 2g, Protein: 4g, Fat: 4g, Sodium: 150mg

Tips:

- Choose low-sodium mozzarella cheese: Look for brands labeled "low sodium" or "reduced sodium" to keep sodium intake in check.
- Limit prosciutto (optional): Prosciutto is high in sodium and fat, so consider using it sparingly or omitting it altogether.
- Portion control: Be mindful of portion sizes, especially if other carbohydrate-rich options are available at the party.

Grilled Chicken with Lemon-Herb Marinade

Prep Time: 15 minutes | **Cooking Time**: 20-25 minutes | **Total Time**: 35-40 minutes | **Servings**: 4

Ingredients:
- 4 boneless, skinless chicken breasts or thighs
- 1/4 cup freshly squeezed lemon juice
- 2 tablespoons olive oil
- 1 tablespoon Dijon mustard
- 1 tablespoon chopped fresh rosemary
- 1 tablespoon chopped fresh thyme
- 1/2 teaspoon dried oregano
- 1/4 teaspoon garlic powder
- 1/4 teaspoon black pepper
- Pinch of salt (optional)
- Skewers (optional)

Directions:
1. Marinate: In a large bowl, whisk together lemon juice, olive oil, Dijon mustard, rosemary, thyme, oregano, garlic powder, and black pepper. Season with salt to taste, if desired.
2. Place chicken breasts or thighs in the marinade, ensuring they are evenly coated. Cover and refrigerate for at least 30 minutes, or up to 4 hours for deeper flavor.
3. Preheat Grill: Prepare your grill for medium-high heat. If using skewers, thread the marinated chicken onto them.
4. Grill: Grill the chicken for 15-20 minutes per side, or until cooked through and juices run clear. Internal temperature should reach 165°F (74°C).
5. Serve: Allow chicken to rest for a few minutes before serving. Enjoy with grilled vegetables, a side salad, or whole-wheat rolls.

Nutritional Information: Calories: 250, Carbohydrates: 5g, Protein: 35g, Fat: 10g, Sodium: 200mg

Tips:
- For a thicker marinade, add a tablespoon of Greek yogurt or low-fat mayonnaise.
- Use boneless, skinless chicken thighs for a juicier result.
- If you don't have fresh herbs, use 1 teaspoon each of dried rosemary, thyme, and oregano.
- Grill vegetables like bell peppers, zucchini, and onions alongside the chicken for a complete meal.
- Serve with a diabetes-friendly dipping sauce like a Greek yogurt-based tzatziki or a simple vinaigrette.
- Monitor portion sizes, especially for carbohydrates depending on additional sides served.

Cauliflower Rice Pilaf

Prep Time: 10 minutes | **Cooking Time**: 20 minutes | **Total Time**: 30 minutes | **Serving Size**: 4-6

Ingredients:

- 1 head cauliflower, riced (about 4 cups)
- 1 tablespoon olive oil
- 1 medium onion, diced
- 2 cloves garlic, minced
- 1/2 teaspoon ground cumin
- 1/4 teaspoon ground turmeric
- 1/4 teaspoon ground coriander
- 1/8 teaspoon cayenne pepper (optional)
- 1 cup vegetable broth
- 1/4 cup chopped fresh parsley
- Salt and pepper to taste
- Optional Additions:
- 1/4 cup chopped pecans or walnuts, toasted
- 1/4 cup crumbled feta cheese
- 1/4 cup sun-dried tomatoes, chopped
- 1/4 cup chopped fresh herbs (mint, cilantro, etc.)

Directions:

1. Heat olive oil in a large skillet over medium heat. Add onion and cook until softened, about 5 minutes.
2. Stir in garlic, cumin, turmeric, coriander, and cayenne pepper (if using). Cook for another minute, until fragrant.
3. Add cauliflower rice and cook for 5 minutes, stirring occasionally.
4. Pour in vegetable broth and bring to a simmer. Reduce heat, cover, and cook for 10 minutes, or until cauliflower rice is tender.
5. Remove from heat and stir in parsley, salt, and pepper to taste.
6. Serve immediately, garnished with your desired optional additions.

Nutritional Information: Calories: 150, Carbohydrates: 15g, Fat: 7g, Protein: 5g, Fiber: 5g, Sodium: 300mg

Tips:

- Use a food processor to easily rice the cauliflower.
- For a richer flavor, use chicken broth instead of vegetable broth.
- Adjust the spices to your liking.
- This dish can be served warm or cold.
- Leftovers can be stored in an airtight container in the refrigerator for up to 3 days.

Roasted Asparagus with Parmesan

Prep Time: 5 minutes | **Cooking Time**: 10-12 minutes | **Total Time**: 15-17 minutes | **Servings**: 2-3

Ingredients:

- 1 pound asparagus, trimmed and ends removed
- 1 tablespoon olive oil
- 1/4 teaspoon salt
- 1/4 teaspoon black pepper
- 1/4 cup grated Parmesan cheese

Directions:

1. Preheat oven to 400°F (200°C). Line a baking sheet with parchment paper.
2. In a large bowl, toss asparagus with olive oil, salt, and pepper. Spread evenly on the prepared baking sheet.
3. Roast for 10-12 minutes, or until tender-crisp, flipping halfway through.
4. Remove from the oven and sprinkle with Parmesan cheese. Serve immediately.

Nutritional Information: Calories: 50, Carbohydrates: 4g, Fiber: 2g, Sugar: 2g, Fat: 1g, Sodium: 70mg

Tips:

- For a more flavorful kick, add a pinch of red pepper flakes or garlic powder to the seasoning mix.

- If you prefer softer asparagus, roast for an additional 2-3 minutes.

- To make this a more festive appetizer, serve the asparagus spears with a low-fat yogurt dip or hummus.

- For a larger group, simply double or triple the recipe.

Quinoa Salad with Feta and Cherry Tomatoes

Prep Time: 15 minutes | **Cooking Time**: 15 minutes | **Total Time**: 30 minutes | **Serving Size**: 4-6

Ingredients:
- 1 cup quinoa, rinsed
- 1 1/2 cups vegetable broth
- 1/2 cup crumbled feta cheese
- 1 cup cherry tomatoes, halved
- 1/2 cucumber, diced
- 1/4 red onion, finely chopped
- 1/4 cup fresh parsley, chopped
- 2 tablespoons olive oil
- 1 tablespoon lemon juice
- 1/2 teaspoon dried oregano
- Salt and pepper to taste

Directions:
1. Cook the quinoa: In a saucepan, combine rinsed quinoa and vegetable broth. Bring to a boil, then reduce heat and simmer for 15 minutes, or until quinoa is fluffy and cooked through. Fluff with a fork and set aside to cool slightly.
2. Prepare the ingredients: While the quinoa cools, crumble the feta cheese, halve the cherry tomatoes, dice the cucumber, finely chop the red onion, and chop the parsley.
3. Assemble the salad: In a large bowl, combine the cooled quinoa, feta cheese, cherry tomatoes, cucumber, red onion, and parsley.
4. Make the dressing: In a small bowl, whisk together olive oil, lemon juice, oregano, salt, and pepper to taste.
5. Dress the salad: Pour the dressing over the salad and toss gently to coat all ingredients evenly.
6. Serve: Enjoy the salad immediately or refrigerate for up to 2 days.

Nutritional Information: Calories: 300, Carbohydrates: 35g, Fiber: 5g, Protein: 10g, Fat: 12g, Saturated Fat: 4g, Sodium: 300mg

Tips:
- For a heartier salad, add cooked grilled chicken or fish.
- To make the salad vegan, omit the feta cheese and use a plant-based dressing.
- If you don't have vegetable broth, you can use water instead.
- Adjust the amount of feta cheese to your preference.
- To reduce sodium, use low-sodium feta cheese or omit it altogether.
- Feel free to customize the salad with other vegetables you like, such as bell peppers, celery, or olives.

Sugar-Free Cheesecake with Berry Compote

Prep Time: 20 minutes | **Cooking Time**: 50 minutes | **Total Time**: 1 hour 10 minutes | **Servings**: 8

Ingredients:

For the Crust:
- 1 1/2 cups almond flour
- 1/4 cup melted butter
- 2 tablespoons erythritol or other sugar substitute
- 1/4 teaspoon ground cinnamon

For the Filling:
- 16 ounces Neufchatel cheese, softened
- 3 large eggs
- 1/2 cup unsweetened almond milk
- 1/4 cup erythritol or other sugar substitute
- 1 tablespoon lemon juice
- 1 teaspoon vanilla extract
- 1/4 teaspoon xanthan gum

For the Berry Compote:
- 2 cups mixed berries (fresh or frozen)
- 1/4 cup water
- 1 tablespoon erythritol or other sugar substitute (optional)
- 1 tablespoon lemon juice
- 1 teaspoon cornstarch

Directions:
1. Prepare the Crust: Preheat oven to 350°F (175°C). Combine almond flour, melted butter, erythritol, and cinnamon in a bowl. Press the mixture into the bottom of a greased 9-inch springform pan. Bake for 10 minutes, then let cool.
2. Make the Filling: In a large bowl, beat together Neufchatel cheese, eggs, almond milk, erythritol, lemon juice, vanilla extract, and xanthan gum until smooth. Pour the filling over the cooled crust.
3. Bake the Cheesecake: Bake for 50 minutes, or until the center is set. Let the cheesecake cool completely in the oven with the door slightly ajar, then refrigerate for at least 4 hours, or overnight.
4. Prepare the Berry Compote: In a saucepan, combine berries, water, erythritol (if using), and lemon juice. Bring to a simmer over medium heat and cook for 5-10 minutes, or until the berries soften and release their juices. In a small bowl, whisk together cornstarch with 1 tablespoon of water. Mix the cornstarch slurry into the simmering berries and cook for 1 minute more, stirring constantly, until the sauce thickens. Let the compote cool slightly.
5. Assemble and Serve: Top the chilled cheesecake with the berry compote and slice into 8 pieces. Serve chilled and enjoy

Nutritional Information: Calories: 250, Carbohydrates: 15g, Fiber: 5g, Fat: 12g, Protein: 8g

Tips:
- For a richer flavor, use full-fat cream cheese instead of Neufchatel.
- If you don't have xanthan gum, you can omit it, but the filling may be slightly less stable.
- You can experiment with different types of berries for the compote.
- To make the cheesecake ahead of time, bake it, cool it completely, then wrap it tightly and freeze for up to 3 months. Thaw overnight in the refrigerator before serving.

NEW YEAR'S EVE CELEBRATION

Spicy Shrimp Ceviche with Citrus and Herbs

Prep Time: 15 minutes | **Cooking Time**: None | **Total Time**: 15 minutes | **Servings**: 4

Ingredients:
- 1 pound raw shrimp, peeled and deveined
- 1/2 cup freshly squeezed lime juice
- 1/4 cup freshly squeezed orange juice
- 1/4 cup finely chopped red onion
- 1/4 cup chopped cilantro
- 1 jalapeno pepper, seeded and finely chopped (optional, for more spice)
- 1/2 avocado, diced
- 1/4 cup chopped cucumber
- 1/4 cup chopped roma tomato
- 1 tablespoon olive oil
- Salt and freshly ground black pepper to taste

1. **Directions**:
2. In a large bowl, combine the lime juice, orange juice, red onion, cilantro, jalapeno (if using), and avocado.
3. Add the shrimp and toss gently to coat.
4. Cover and refrigerate for at least 30 minutes, or until the shrimp are opaque and cooked through.
5. Stir in the cucumber, tomato, olive oil, salt, and pepper.
6. Serve immediately with your favorite low-carb crackers or tostadas.

Nutritional information: Calories: 200, Carbohydrates: 10g, Fiber: 2g, Sugar: 5g, Protein: 20g, Fat: 5g, Sodium: 200mg

Tips:
- For a more flavorful ceviche, marinate the shrimp for longer, up to 2 hours.
- If you don't have fresh citrus juice, you can use bottled juice, but the flavor won't be as bright.
- Be careful not to overcook the shrimp, as they will become tough.
- You can adjust the amount of jalapeno pepper to your desired level of spiciness.
- Serve with a variety of colorful chopped vegetables for added flavor and nutrients.

Herb-Crusted Salmon Fillets

Prep Time: 10 minutes | **Cooking Time**: 15-20 minutes | **Total Time**: 25-30 minutes | **Servings**: 2

Ingredients:
- 2 salmon fillets (6-8 oz each)
- 1 tablespoon olive oil
- 1/4 cup chopped fresh herbs (such as dill, parsley, chives, thyme)
- 1/4 teaspoon dried oregano
- 1/4 teaspoon garlic powder
- 1/4 teaspoon onion powder
- Salt and pepper to taste
- 1/4 cup panko breadcrumbs (optional, use crushed nuts for a lower-carb option)
- 1 lemon, sliced (optional, for garnish)

Directions:
1. Preheat oven to 400°F (200°C). Line a baking sheet with parchment paper.
2. Pat the salmon fillets dry with paper towels. Drizzle with olive oil and season with salt and pepper.
3. In a small bowl, combine chopped herbs, oregano, garlic powder, and onion powder.
4. Sprinkle the herb mixture evenly over the salmon fillets, pressing gently to adhere.
5. Optional: Top with panko breadcrumbs for a crispy crust.
6. Place the salmon on the prepared baking sheet and bake for 15-20 minutes, or until cooked through and opaque.
7. Garnish with lemon slices (optional) and serve immediately.

   Nutritional Information: Calories: 350, Protein: 35g, Fat: 15g, Carbs: 10g, Sodium: 300mg

Tips:
- Use a variety of your favorite fresh herbs for the crust.
- For a lower-carb option, skip the panko breadcrumbs and use crushed nuts (almonds, pecans) for the crust.
- Serve the salmon with roasted vegetables or a side salad for a complete meal.
- Be mindful of portion sizes and choose low-sodium soy sauce when making the recipe.
- For added flavor, you can marinate the salmon in a mixture of olive oil, lemon juice, and your favorite herbs for 30 minutes before baking.

Zucchini Noodles with Pesto

Prep Time: 10 minutes | **Cooking Time**: 10 minutes | **Total Time**: 20 minutes | **Serving Size**: 2

Ingredients:

- 2 medium zucchinis, spiralized
- 1/2 cup prepared pesto (choose a low-sugar or sugar-free option)
- 1/4 cup cherry tomatoes, halved
- 1/4 cup crumbled feta cheese
- 1/4 cup chopped fresh basil
- 1 tablespoon olive oil
- Salt and pepper to taste

Directions:

1. Spiralize the zucchinis: Use a spiralizer to create long, thin zucchini noodles. If you don't have a spiralizer, you can use a julienne peeler or mandoline to create thin ribbons.
2. Cook the zucchini noodles (optional): This step is optional, as zucchini noodles can be enjoyed raw. However, if you prefer them warm, heat the olive oil in a large skillet over medium heat. Add the zucchini noodles and cook for 2-3 minutes, stirring frequently, until slightly softened.
3. Assemble the dish: In a large bowl, combine the cooked zucchini noodles (if using), pesto, cherry tomatoes, feta cheese, and basil. Toss gently to coat everything evenly.
4. Season and serve: Season with salt and pepper to taste. Serve immediately and enjoy

Nutritional Information: Calories: 250, Carbohydrates: 15g, Fiber: 4g, Net Carbs: 11g, Fat: 15g, Protein: 8g

Tips:

- For added protein, you can include grilled chicken or shrimp.
- To make the dish vegan, use vegan pesto and omit the feta cheese.
- If you don't have fresh basil, you can use 1 teaspoon dried basil.
- Leftover zucchini noodles can be stored in an airtight container in the refrigerator for up to 2 days.

Roasted Balsamic Brussels sprouts

Prep Time: 10 minutes | **Cooking Time**: 20-25 minutes | **Total Time**: 30-35 minutes | **Servings**: 4-6

Ingredients:

- 1 pound Brussels sprouts, trimmed and halved
- 2 tablespoons olive oil
- 1 tablespoon balsamic vinegar
- 1/2 teaspoon Dijon mustard
- 1/4 teaspoon dried thyme
- 1/4 teaspoon garlic powder
- Salt and pepper to taste
- Optional: Balsamic glaze, chopped fresh herbs (parsley, thyme, or rosemary) for garnish

Directions:
1. Preheat oven to 400°F (200°C). Line a baking sheet with parchment paper.
2. In a large bowl, toss Brussels sprouts with olive oil, balsamic vinegar, Dijon mustard, thyme, garlic powder, salt, and pepper.
3. Spread Brussels sprouts evenly on the prepared baking sheet.
4. Roast for 20-25 minutes, or until tender and slightly browned, flipping halfway through.
5. (Optional) Drizzle with balsamic glaze and garnish with chopped herbs before serving.

Nutritional Information: Calories: 70, Carbohydrates: 10g, Fiber: 3g, Sugar: 5g, Fat: 4g, Protein: 2g

Tips:

- For a sweeter flavor, add a sprinkle of brown sugar or maple syrup to the balsamic glaze.
- If you don't have Dijon mustard, you can substitute it with yellow mustard.
- Make sure to cut the Brussels sprouts into similar sizes so they cook evenly.
- Don't overcrowd the baking sheet, as this will prevent the Brussels sprouts from roasting properly.
- You can roast the Brussels sprouts ahead of time and reheat them before serving.

Quinoa and Kale Stuffed Bell Peppers

Prep Time: 15 minutes | **Cooking Time**: 45 minutes | **Total Time**: 60 minutes | **Servings**: 4

Ingredients:

- 4 large bell peppers (any color)
- 1 cup uncooked quinoa, rinsed
- 1 1/2 cups vegetable broth
- 1 tablespoon olive oil
- 1 medium onion, chopped
- 2 cloves garlic, minced
- 4 cups kale, roughly chopped
- 1/2 cup crumbled feta cheese (optional)
- 1/4 cup chopped fresh parsley
- 1/4 teaspoon dried thyme
- Salt and black pepper to taste

Directions:
1. Preheat oven to 375°F (190°C).
2. Prepare the bell peppers: Wash and halve the bell peppers lengthwise, removing the seeds and membranes. Place them in a baking dish cut-side up.
3. Cook the quinoa: In a saucepan, combine the quinoa and vegetable broth. Bring to a boil, then reduce heat, cover, and simmer for 15 minutes, or until the quinoa is cooked and fluffy. Fluff with a fork and set aside.
4. Sauté the vegetables: Heat olive oil in a large skillet over medium heat. Add the onion and cook until softened, about 5 minutes. Add the garlic and cook for another minute, until fragrant.
5. Add the kale and cook until wilted, about 5 minutes. Season with salt and pepper.
6. Assemble the stuffed peppers: Divide the cooked quinoa among the bell pepper halves. Top with the kale mixture and sprinkle with feta cheese (if using).
7. Bake for 25-30 minutes, or until the bell peppers are tender and the filling is heated through.
8. Garnish with fresh parsley and serve immediately.

Nutritional Information: Calories: 350, Carbohydrates: 35g, Fiber: 8g, Protein: 15g, Fat: 10g, Sodium: 300mg

Tips:

- For a vegetarian option, omit the feta cheese.
- You can add other vegetables to the filling, such as diced tomatoes, zucchini, or mushrooms.
- To make the dish ahead of time, assemble the stuffed peppers and bake them up to 24 hours in advance. Reheat before serving.
- Serve with a side of roasted vegetables or a green salad for a complete meal.

Dark Chocolate-Dipped Strawberries

Prep Time: 10 minutes | **Cooking Time**: 0 minutes | **Total Time**: 10 minutes | **Serving Size**: 12

Ingredients:
- 12 large, fresh strawberries, washed and patted dry
- 4 oz. dark chocolate (70% cacao or higher), chopped
- 1 Tbsp. coconut oil (optional, for a thinner chocolate coating)
- 1/4 cup chopped nuts, seeds, or sprinkles (optional, for garnish)

1. **Directions**:
2. Prepare the strawberries: Make sure the strawberries are clean, dry, and at room temperature. Hull them carefully, leaving a small bit of the green stem attached for presentation.
3. Melt the chocolate: In a small microwave-safe bowl, melt the chocolate in 30-second intervals, stirring in between, until smooth and melted. You can also melt the chocolate over a double boiler using low heat.
4. Optional thinning: If desired, add the coconut oil to the melted chocolate and stir until well combined. This will make the chocolate coating thinner and easier to dip.
5. Dip the strawberries: Holding the strawberry by the stem, dip it into the melted chocolate, coating it about halfway up. Allow excess chocolate to drip off, then gently tap the strawberry against the bowl to remove any drips.
6. Garnish (optional): Immediately dip the coated strawberry in your chosen garnish (nuts, seeds, sprinkles) before the chocolate sets. Alternatively, you can drizzle some melted chocolate over the top for a decorative touch.
7. Chill and serve: Place the dipped strawberries on a parchment-lined baking sheet and refrigerate for at least 30 minutes, or until the chocolate is set. Serve chilled

Nutritional Information: Calories: 80, Carbohydrates: 12g, Fiber: 2g, Sugar: 8g, Fat: 4g, Saturated Fat: 2g, Protein: 1g, Sodium: 2mg

Tips:
- Use high-quality, dark chocolate with at least 70% cacao content for the most health benefits and intense flavor.
- If you don't have coconut oil, you can use a small amount of vegetable oil instead, but it will alter the taste slightly.
- Be careful not to over-dip the strawberries, as this can lead to excess sugar and calories.
- For a festive touch, use red and white sprinkles or chopped pistachios for garnish.
- If you have a little more time, you can temper the chocolate for a smoother, shinier finish.
- Serve the strawberries with a small glass of sparkling water or unsweetened tea for a refreshing treat.

LIFESTYLE AND EXERCISE

Maintaining a healthy lifestyle and including regular exercise is vital for persons with diabetes. Here are lifestyle and exercise strategies to help regulate blood sugar levels and boost overall well-being:

LIFESTYLE TIPS

Regular Monitoring:

- Monitor blood glucose levels frequently to learn how various diets and activities impact them.

Healthy Eating Habits:

- Follow a balanced and healthy diet rich in fruits, vegetables, lean meats, and whole grains.
- Choose meals with a low glycemic index to help regulate blood sugar levels.

Portion Control:

- Be cautious of portion sizes to prevent overeating and limit calorie intake.

Hydration:

- Stay well-hydrated by drinking lots of water throughout the day.

Regular Sleep:

- Aim for 7-9 hours of excellent sleep every night to improve general health and blood sugar management.

Stress Management:

- Practice stress-reducing strategies such as meditation, deep breathing, or yoga.
- Engage in activities you like to encourage relaxation.

Regular Medical Check-ups:

- Schedule frequent check-ups with healthcare specialists to assess general health and diabetes treatment.

Limit Alcohol and Quit Smoking:

➢ Limit alcohol consumption and avoid smoking to decrease further health hazards.

Social Support:

➢ Build a support network of friends, family, or a diabetic support group to share experiences and suggestions.

Education and Empowerment:

➢ Stay educated about diabetes management via education programs or conversations with healthcare specialists.
➢ Take an active part in controlling your diabetes and advocate for your health needs.

Consult with Healthcare Professionals:

➢ Consult with healthcare specialists, including a doctor and a fitness expert, before beginning a new workout plan.

EXERCISE

Regular Exercise:

➢ Aim for at least 150 minutes of moderate-intensity aerobic activity every week.
➢ Include a range of workouts such as walking, swimming, cycling, or dancing.

Strength Training:

➢ Incorporate strength training activities at least two days a week to grow and maintain muscular mass.

Flexibility and Balance Exercises:

➢ Include flexibility and balance activities, such as yoga or tai chi, to promote general well-being.

Consistency is Key:

➢ Establish a steady fitness program to make it a sustainable part of your lifestyle.

Post-Meal Walking:

- ➢ Take brief walks after meals to help reduce blood sugar levels.
- ➢ Consider a post-dinner walk to aid digestion.

Monitor Blood Sugar Levels during Exercise:

- ➢ Check blood sugar levels before, during, and after exercise to evaluate its influence.
- ➢ Carry fast-acting carbs in case of low blood sugar (hypoglycemia) during exercise.

Stay Hydrated:

- ➢ Drink water before, during, and after exercise to keep hydrated.

Listen to Your Body:

- ➢ Pay attention to how your body reacts to various kinds and levels of exercise.
- ➢ Adjust your regimen depending on how you feel.

Adapt Exercise Routine:

- ➢ Adapt your workout program depending on changes in health, medication, or other circumstances.
- ➢ Choose activities that you like to make exercise more fun and sustainable.

INCORPORATING PHYSICAL ACTIVITY INTO DAILY LIFE

Incorporating physical exercise into everyday life is vital for general health and well-being. For people, particularly those managing diabetes, regular physical exercise may play a vital role in increasing insulin sensitivity, controlling weight, and lowering the risk of complications. Here are practical strategies for incorporating physical exercise into your everyday routine:

1. **Set Realistic objectives**: Start Small: Begin with attainable objectives, such as a 10-minute walk, and gradually increase time and effort.

2. **Choose Activities You Enjoy**: Find Pleasure in Exercise: Engage in activities you like to make them more sustainable and pleasurable.

3. **Schedule Regular Breaks**: Take brief Breaks: Set reminders to get up, stretch, or take a brief walk every hour, particularly if you have sedentary work.

4. **Walk wherever Possible**: Choose Walking: Opt for walking wherever practicable - take the stairs, park further away, or walk to nearby locations.

5. **Involve Family and Friends**: Make It Social: Encourage family or friends to join you for activities, making it more pleasurable and developing a support system.

6. **Utilize Active transit**: riding or Walking: Consider riding or walking for short excursions instead of depending on motorized transit.

7. **Incorporate Exercise into Daily** Tasks: Household Chores: Make domestic duties more active, such as gardening, vacuuming, or cleaning.

8. **Join Fitness Classes or Groups**:
Community Engagement: Participate in local fitness courses or join a club, building social relationships while keeping active.

9. **Embrace Technology**: Fitness applications: Use applications that give training plans, measure your progress, and provide inspiration.

10. **Make It a routine**: Consistency is Key: Set a constant time for exercise, making it a daily or weekly routine.

11. **Explore Different Activities: Variety**: Keep things interesting by attempting other hobbies like swimming, dancing, or yoga.

12. **Regular a pattern**: Establish a Routine: Having a regular pattern makes it simpler to include physical exercise into your everyday life.

13. **Take Advantage of Nature**: Outdoor Activities: Explore outdoor activities like hiking, bicycling, or running in parks or natural environments.

14. **Incorporate Strength Training**: Resistance activities: Include strength training activities at least twice a week to build muscular strength.

15. **Split up Long Bouts**: Short Bursts of Activity: If time is a problem, split up your activity into shorter bouts throughout the day.

16. **Stay Hydrated**: Water Breaks: Stay hydrated throughout strenuous exercise, particularly in warmer weather.

17. **Invest in Home Exercise Equipment**: Basic Equipment: Consider basic home exercise equipment, such as resistance bands or dumbbells, for convenience.
18. **Track Your Progress**: Monitor Achievements: Keep a log of your physical activities to measure improvement and remain motivated.
19. **Consult with Healthcare Professionals**: Seek Professional Advice: Consult with healthcare professionals or fitness experts to build a safe and effective workout regimen.

20. **Listen to Your Body**: Adapt to Your Body: Be conscious of your body's signals and modify your exercise level appropriately.

CONCLUSION

The Complete Diabetes Diet Cookbook" provides a thorough reference for anyone seeking not just tasty and gratifying dishes but also practical insights into treating diabetes via diet. The cookbook digs into the complexity of diabetes, offering a grasp of the illness, its influence on the body, and the importance of diet in achieving optimum health.

The cookbook starts by unraveling the principles of diabetes, giving insights into the illness, and cultivating a thorough grasp of the need for a balanced diet in diabetes care. From the foundations of diabetic nutrition to the subtleties of designing a balanced plate and making healthy meals, the cookbook provides a comprehensive approach to equip people with the information and skills required for optimal diabetes management.

The addition of the Plate Method, Glycemic Index, and Glycemic Load adds a practical dimension, allowing readers real tools to make educated dietary choices that fit with blood sugar control objectives. Emphasizing the influence of various meals on blood sugar levels, the cookbook advocates a thorough and tailored approach to nutritional planning.

Highlighting key nutrients for those with diabetes, the cookbook includes a deep analysis of fiber, protein, healthy fats, vitamins, minerals, and other critical components. The focus on balanced meals not only promotes blood sugar regulation but also adds to general well-being.

Moreover, the cookbook goes beyond the area of food, including helpful information on kitchen needs, shopping recommendations, and practical methods to integrate physical exercise into everyday life. It emphasizes the necessity of a holistic approach to diabetes treatment, embracing not just food choices but also lifestyle aspects that play a crucial role in attaining optimum health.

In essence, "The Complete Diabetes Diet Cookbook" is more than simply a collection of recipes; it is a comprehensive resource that encourages people to take care of their health. By combining culinary inventiveness with evidence-based nutritional advice, the cookbook presents a blueprint for adopting a diabetes-friendly lifestyle that is both fulfilling and fun. As people begin their culinary adventure with this cookbook in hand, they learn not only a repertoire of tasty recipes but also a deeper awareness of how to make thoughtful and health-conscious decisions that may positively influence their lives.

FREQUENTLY ASKED QUESTIONS

1. **What is Diabetes?**
Answer: Diabetes is a chronic health condition that occurs when the body cannot produce enough insulin or effectively use the insulin it produces. Insulin is a hormone that regulates blood sugar (glucose) levels.

2. **What are the Types of Diabetes?**
Answer: There are primarily three types of diabetes: Type 1 diabetes, Type 2 diabetes, and gestational diabetes. Type 1 diabetes is an autoimmune condition where the body attacks and destroys insulin-producing cells. Type 2 diabetes occurs when the body becomes resistant to insulin or doesn't produce enough. Gestational diabetes develops during pregnancy.

3. **How is Diabetes Diagnosed?**
Answer: Diabetes is diagnosed through blood tests that measure blood sugar levels. Common tests include fasting blood sugar, oral glucose tolerance test, and A1c test, which reflects average blood sugar levels over the past 2-3 months.

4. **What is Prediabetes?**
Answer: Prediabetes is a condition where blood sugar levels are higher than normal but not yet high enough to be diagnosed as diabetes. It is a warning sign that individuals are at risk of developing Type 2 diabetes.

5. **What Role Does Diet Play in Diabetes Management?**
Answer: Diet plays a crucial role in diabetes management. Consuming a balanced diet that includes whole grains, lean proteins, healthy fats, and plenty of fruits and vegetables helps regulate blood sugar levels.

6. **What is the Glycemic Index (GI)?**
Answer: The Glycemic Index (GI) is a scale that ranks carbohydrate-containing foods based on their impact on blood sugar levels. Low-GI foods have a slower impact, while high-GI foods cause a rapid spike in blood sugar.

7. **Can People with Diabetes Eat Sweets?**
Answer: While individuals with diabetes can enjoy sweets in moderation, it's essential to monitor portion sizes and consider the overall carbohydrate content. It's advisable to choose healthier sweet options or use sugar substitutes.

8. What is the Plate Method?

Answer: The Plate Method is a visual way to plan meals, focusing on portion control and a balanced mix of carbohydrates, proteins, and non-starchy vegetables. It involves filling half the plate with non-starchy vegetables, a quarter with protein, and a quarter with grains or starchy foods.

9. How important is Physical Activity in Diabetes Management?

Answer: Physical activity is crucial in diabetes management. Regular exercise helps improve insulin sensitivity, lowers blood sugar levels, and supports overall health. Both aerobic exercises and strength training are beneficial.

10. What Should I Consider When Grocery Shopping for Diabetes?

Answer: When grocery shopping for diabetes, consider choosing whole, unprocessed foods, checking nutritional labels, and prioritizing whole grains, lean proteins, and healthy fats. Be mindful of portion sizes and limit processed and sugary foods.

11. Can Diabetes Be Prevented?

Answer: Type 1 diabetes cannot be prevented, but Type 2 diabetes can often be delayed or prevented through lifestyle modifications such as maintaining a healthy diet, regular physical activity, and weight management.

12. What is the Role of Medications in Diabetes Management?

Answer: Medications for diabetes management vary and may include insulin, oral medications, or injectables. The choice depends on the type of diabetes and individual health needs.

13. How Often Should Blood Sugar Levels Be Monitored?

Answer: The frequency of blood sugar monitoring depends on individual treatment plans. Some may need to monitor several times a day, while others may do so less frequently. Regular monitoring helps track how well treatment plans are working.

14. What are Hypoglycemia and Hyperglycemia?

Answer: Hypoglycemia is low blood sugar, which can result in symptoms such as shakiness, sweating, and confusion. Hyperglycemia is high blood sugar, leading to symptoms like increased thirst, frequent urination, and fatigue.

15. Can Alcohol Be Consumed with Diabetes?

Answer: Alcohol can be consumed in moderation, but it's important to be mindful of its impact on blood sugar levels. Consuming alcohol without food can lead to hypoglycemia, and alcoholic beverages can contribute to overall calorie intake.

16. **How Does Stress Affect Diabetes?**
Answer: Stress can affect blood sugar levels by triggering the release of hormones like cortisol. Managing stress through relaxation techniques, exercise, and adequate sleep is important for overall diabetes care.

17. **Is Diabetes Hereditary?**
Answer: There is a genetic component to diabetes. While having a family history increases the risk, lifestyle factors also play a significant role. Not everyone with a family history will develop diabetes, and some without a family history may still develop the condition.

18. **Are There Specific Diets for Diabetes?**
Answer: There is no one-size-fits-all diet for diabetes. However, a balanced diet that focuses on whole, nutrient-dense foods, portion control, and individualized meal planning is generally recommended.

19. **How Does Smoking Affect Diabetes?**
Answer: Smoking is associated with an increased risk of Type 2 diabetes and can worsen diabetes complications. Quitting smoking is beneficial for overall health and diabetes management.

20. **Can Children Develop Diabetes?**
Answer: Yes, children can develop diabetes. While Type 1 diabetes is more common in children, there has been an increase in the prevalence of Type 2 diabetes in younger individuals, often associated with lifestyle factors.

GLOSSARY

A1C (HbA1c):
Definition: A measure of average blood glucose levels over the past 2-3 months. It is expressed as a percentage and is a key indicator of long-term glucose control.

Blood Glucose:
Definition: The amount of glucose (sugar) present in the blood. It is measured in milligrams per deciliter (mg/dL) or millimoles per liter (mmol/L).

Carbohydrates:
Definition: One of the three main macronutrients, along with fats and proteins. Carbohydrates include sugars, starches, and fibers and have a direct impact on blood sugar levels.

Insulin:
Definition: A hormone produced by the pancreas that facilitates the uptake of glucose from the bloodstream into cells, helping to regulate blood sugar levels.

Glucose Meter:
Definition: A device used to measure blood glucose levels at a specific moment. Users typically prick a finger to obtain a small blood sample, which is then analyzed by the meter.

Glycemic Index (GI):
Definition: A scale that ranks carbohydrates based on their impact on blood sugar levels. Foods with a higher GI Cause a more rapid increase in blood glucose.

Glycemic Load (GL):
Definition: A measure that takes into account both the quality and quantity of carbohydrates in a specific serving of food, providing a more accurate representation of its impact on blood sugar.

Ketones:
Definition: Substances produced when the body breaks down fat for energy in the absence of sufficient insulin. High levels of ketones can be a sign of diabetic ketoacidosis (DKA).

Pancreas:
Definition: An organ located behind the stomach that produces insulin and other digestive enzymes. Dysfunction of the pancreas can lead to diabetes.

Prediabetes:
Definition: A condition where blood sugar levels are higher than normal but not yet high enough for a diabetes diagnosis. It is a warning sign of increased diabetes risk.

Type 1 Diabetes:
Definition: An autoimmune condition where the immune system attacks and destroys insulin-producing cells in the pancreas, leading to a lack of insulin.

Type 2 Diabetes:
Definition: A condition where the body becomes resistant to insulin or does not produce enough insulin to maintain normal blood sugar levels.

Hyperglycemia:
Definition: High blood sugar levels, often resulting from insufficient insulin or insulin resistance. It can lead to symptoms such as increased thirst, frequent urination, and fatigue.

Hypoglycemia:
Definition: Low blood sugar levels, often caused by too much insulin, skipping meals, or engaging in excessive physical activity. It can result in symptoms such as shakiness, confusion, and sweating.

Metabolism:
Definition: The set of chemical processes that occur within the body to convert food into energy. Impaired metabolism is often associated with diabetes.

Peripheral Neuropathy:
Definition: Nerve damage that commonly affects the feet and legs, leading to tingling, numbness, and pain. It is a common complication of diabetes.

Retinopathy:
Definition: Damage to the blood vessels in the retina of the eye, often leading to vision problems. It is a complication of diabetes.

Polyphagia, Polydipsia, Polyuria:
Definitions:
Polyphagia: Excessive hunger.
Polydipsia: Excessive thirst.
Polyuria: Excessive urination.

Relation to Diabetes: These symptoms can be signs of diabetes, particularly when accompanied by other indicators.

Acanthosis Nigricans:
Definition: A skin condition characterized by dark, velvety patches, often occurring in body folds. It can be associated with insulin resistance and Type 2 diabetes.

Basal Rate:
Definition: The continuous, background insulin delivery provided by an insulin pump to maintain stable blood sugar levels between meals and overnight.

Bolus:
Definition: An additional dose of insulin taken to cover the rise in blood sugar levels that occurs after meals or to correct high blood sugar.

C-Peptide:
Definition: A byproduct of insulin production. Measuring C-peptide levels can help determine the amount of insulin the pancreas is producing.

Diabetes Educator:
Definition: A healthcare professional, often a nurse or dietitian, specializing in diabetes education. They guide managing diabetes, including self-care, nutrition, and medication.

Gestational Diabetes:
Definition: Diabetes that develops during pregnancy. It increases the risk of complications for both the mother and baby.

Glucagon:
Definition: A hormone produced by the pancreas that raises blood sugar levels by stimulating the liver to convert stored glycogen into glucose.

Hemoglobin A1C (HbA1c):
Definition: See A1C. It is a long-term indicator of blood glucose levels.

Insulin Pump:
Definition: A device worn externally that delivers a continuous supply of insulin through a small tube inserted under the skin. It can also provide additional insulin as needed.

LADA (Latent Autoimmune Diabetes in Adults):
Definition: A form of Type 1 diabetes that develops in adulthood. It is characterized by the gradual onset of autoimmune destruction of insulin-producing cells.

Microalbuminuria:
Definition: The presence of a slightly elevated level of albumin (a protein) in the urine, indicating early kidney damage. It is a complication of diabetes.

Neuropathy:
Definition: Nerve damage that can cause pain, tingling, and numbness, commonly affecting the hands and feet. Peripheral neuropathy is a common complication of diabetes.

Oral Glucose Tolerance Test (OGTT):
Definition: A diagnostic test in which blood sugar levels are measured before and after consuming a glucose solution. It helps assess how the body processes glucose.

Pancreas Transplant:
Definition: A surgical procedure where a healthy pancreas is transplanted into a person with diabetes. It can restore normal insulin production.

Postprandial:
Definition: Refers to the time after eating a meal. Postprandial blood sugar levels are measured to assess the impact of food on glucose levels.

Renal Threshold:
Definition: The blood glucose level at which the kidneys begin to excrete excess glucose into the urine. It is an important concept in understanding kidney function in diabetes.

Sensor-Augmented Pump (SAP):
Definition: An insulin pump that integrates with continuous glucose monitoring (CGM) systems, providing real-time glucose data to help make insulin delivery decisions.

Target Range:
Definition: The ideal blood sugar range that individuals with diabetes aim to maintain. It is often defined by healthcare professionals based on individual health goals.

U-100 Insulin:
Definition: A common concentration of insulin, where each milliliter of insulin contains 100 units.

Visceral Fat:
Definition: Fat stored in the abdominal cavity around internal organs. Excess visceral fat is associated with insulin resistance and an increased risk of Type 2 diabetes.

Printed in Great Britain
by Amazon